When God Doesn't
Answer

When God Doesn't Answer

Removing Roadblocks
to Answered Prayer

Woodrow Kroll

Baker Books

A Division of Baker Book House Co
Grand Rapids, Michigan 49516

Published by Baker Books
a division of Baker Book House Company
P.O. Box 6287, Grand Rapids, MI 49516-6287

Second Printing, March 1997

Printed in the United States of America.

Library of Congress Cataloging-in-Publication Data

Kroll, Woodrow Michael, 1944–
    When God doesn't answer : removing roadblocks to answered prayer / Woodrow Kroll.
      p. cm.
    Includes bibliographical references.
    ISBN 0-8010-5726-4 (paper)
    1. Prayer—Christianity. I. Title.
BV215.K76 1997
248.3′2—dc20   96-19389

For current information about all releases from
Baker Book House, visit our web site:
                              http://www.bakerbooks.com/

To
my praying parents,
Frank and Betty Kroll,
who always
seemed to get answers
from God

Contents

# Preface

For anyone who has read my previous book, *Empowered to Pray*, it is legitimate to ask, "Why another book on prayer?" Actually the two books are not similar in any way. The first book focuses on the potency of prayer; this one focuses on the impotency of the one praying. The first book treats how to get answers to our prayers; this one treats why we sometimes do not get answers. *Empowered to Pray* is solution-oriented, with a few problems thrown in. *When God Doesn't Answer* is problem-oriented, with a few solutions thrown in. Both are necessary, however, because both treat the significance of prayer in the context of a right relationship with God.

In some respects, this book grew out of the first book. The very subject of *Empowered to Pray* necessitated *When God Doesn't Answer*. If you are frustrated by God's silence when you pray, you want to know what's wrong. What is blocking your prayer from reaching his ears, or his answer from reaching your heart? These are the issues grappled with in *When God Doesn't Answer.*

The persons mentioned in this book are real; their names, for the most part, have been changed to insure their anonymity. In a sense, however, they are you and I, for we all have experienced much of what they did in getting answers to our prayers.

Expressing gratitude to the good folks at Baker Book House is always appropriate. Special thanks to Dan Van't Kerkhoff and his team for tackling this second book on prayer on the heels of the first. And thanks to my secretary, Cathy Strate, who faithfully did the tedious work of checking the manuscript again and again. Thanks also to Linda and my family for their support during the months of writing. And of course, thanks to all who listen to the *Back to the Bible* broadcast. You were the first to be exposed to the ideas in this book as they were formulated through the daily course of my broadcasting.

If reading this book will remove the prayer blockers and help you get answers to your prayers, my joy will be full. I pray you will enjoy communion with your heavenly Father, free from the hindrances that discourage you when God doesn't answer.

Introduction

When I pray, coincidences happen, and when I do not, they don't.

William Temple

Christina wrote to me because she needed help. She read in a brochure that I was to speak at a Bible conference in her area and asked if she could talk with me about a personal matter. The conference was months away, but she was willing to wait. I wrote that I would be happy to speak with her.

It was Tuesday. The week of the Bible conference had finally arrived, and my wife, Linda, and I entered the auditorium before the morning service. There she was, a small woman with dark hair. She was timid and at first barely looked my way. I sensed she was embarrassed to speak to me. She had an active, chubby little boy with her who was about eight years old.

Finally she approached. "Hi, I'm Christina. I wrote to you. Do you remember?" I had remembered and greeted her with a smile. "Can you talk with me?" she queried. "Of course," I replied. "Can we wait until after the service? We'll find a quiet place and talk then." She agreed.

The service lasted about an hour and a half. After it was over and most of the people were gone, I spied Christina, patiently waiting for me at the back of the auditorium. We found a room nearby, and Linda and I invited Christina in to talk.

She brought her squirming little guy along. I asked if he belonged to her, and Christina said, "Yes. This is my son Randy." I could see that we had to find something for Randy to do. Fortunately, people were still milling about in the auditorium. We found someone to entertain Randy and got down to business.

Christina immediately broke into tears. She was shy, but the tears flowed freely. As soon as she regained her composure, Christina told us her story. It was a saga I had heard too many times before—the tortured life of a woman who married early, married the wrong man, and married for worse, not for better.

Bob had been unfaithful to Christina right from the start. Not that Christina was unattractive; that doesn't seem to matter to many adulterous husbands. Bob was just irresponsible, uncaring, and self-absorbed. Christina knew he was no good; her mother had warned her about him. But in the beginning Christina had stars in her eyes and palpitations in her heart, and the rest was predictable history.

"Why did you want to meet with me, Christina? Do you want to know what went wrong or whether you have the right to divorce your husband?" I asked these questions because they are usually the ones tearful wives ask. But Christina had another question. Not the "Why did this happen to me?" question, although she had to wonder about that as well. She knew she had acted foolishly and now was paying for that foolishness. Christina stammered, "All I want to know is why doesn't God answer my prayers? I have prayed and prayed that Bob would get his life straightened out, and nothing happens."

Christina's heart cry hits one of the raw nerves of faith. Why doesn't God answer our prayers? Where is he when we need him most?

She continued, "I've talked with my pastor. I've been to a counselor. They keep reassuring me, but I don't think God is listening anymore."

Christina's concerns are repeated hundreds of times a day, every day of the year by hurting wives who wonder what is wrong with them that caused their husband to leave, and who are not a little frustrated because God hasn't done anything about it.

Christina's concerns about unanswered prayer are not unique to hurting wives. Hurting husbands have them too, as do hurting grandmothers, pastors, students, and parents. See if any of these scenarios sound familiar:

"I've been praying for a job. I have good qualifications. I'm willing to work; I need the work. My family and I pray every night that God will give me a job. I go out looking for work every day. But no one wants to hire a fifty-five-year-old who was buried in middle management until his company downsized."

"The ladies at my home Bible study were praying with me that my husband would stop his drinking when he burst through the door as drunk as a skunk. I was so embarrassed. What am I going to do? God just isn't listening."

"My wife has been so depressed lately. Things haven't been too good between us for a long time. Every night I pray that God will pick up her spirits, but now she's talking crazy. She has even threatened suicide. Why doesn't God do something?"

There are common denominators here. In each case, someone prayed; in each case, God did not answer. What does it mean when God doesn't answer our prayers? Isn't he listening to us? Doesn't he care? Maybe he isn't there after all.

If you've ever prayed and God didn't answer, you've probably asked yourself these questions. It's easy to blame God. After all, we can't see him; we can't challenge him and expect a response. If we blame God for unanswered prayer, that gets us off the hook—or does it?

What are the real reasons God doesn't answer? What blocks our prayers? Does God always hear us when we pray? If he always hears, does he always answer? Are we just not tuned in to his answer? What causes unanswered prayer?

As you read what the Bible says about the times when God doesn't answer, you may be surprised. Much of our thinking about unanswered prayer is fuzzy. God is a prayer-hearing and a prayer-answering God, isn't he? Well, not always. The Bible frequently says that God turns his ear away from his people. In fact, occasionally he says, "Don't even bother to pray; I won't listen."

Sometimes we smash face first into a brick wall when we pray. That's when we encounter prayer blockers—attitudes or habits that keep our prayers from being answered, or even heard, by God. We try to hurdle them, but we fall flat on our face. We try to go around them, but we run out of bounds. We can't go under them; we've got to go through them. But first we have to identify them. We have to know what these prayer blockers are, where they are, and sometimes who they are. That's going to take some insight from God's Word.

Donald Bloesch says, "As the omnipotent and omniscient God he hears and knows all prayer, but as the holy One who detests all sin and iniquity he will not give an open ear to prayers that arise out of human arrogance and give glory only to man."[1] If Bloesch is right, we need to swallow hard and see if we are the cause of our unanswered prayers.

What I told Christina that day at the conference is what the Bible tells us every day. God will not always hear our prayers, nor will he always answer. But he really wants to answer. In fact, he is eager to hear from us. "The LORD is near to all who call on him" (Ps. 145:18). So, if you want him to answer, you must discover what it is that's blocking your prayer.

It is not likely that your prayer is being hindered by all the prayer blockers identified in the following pages, but it only takes one to keep you from getting an answer from God. Confronting your prayer blockers is hardly ever enjoyable, but take heart. Peeling them back one at a time will get you to the heart of the problem when God doesn't answer.

Prayer Blocker #1

God doesn't answer when

We Forget to Ask

The great tragedy of life is not unanswered prayer but un-offered prayer.

F. B. Meyer

Think about these words: *exhilarating, electrifying, empowering*. Stimulating aren't they?

What am I talking about—some new multimegabyte computer? No, I'm talking about the feeling that grips us when our prayers are answered. Energizing. Emancipating. Exciting.

Now think about these words: *deflating, disturbing, debilitating*. It's like being kicked in the stomach.

I'm not talking about losing a hard-fought election. I'm talking about the feeling that grips us when our prayers go unanswered. Depleting. Disillusioning. Demoralizing.

There is nothing quite as motivating as answered prayer. When God says yes to our request, we feel like Moses on the mountain, Paul outside the prison, or Peter walking on the water. Prayer is fun when it works. But let one request fall on divine deaf ears and we feel emptied, extinguished, exploited. Unanswered prayer may be the biggest downer in the Christian life. It can lead to depression, despair, and defeat.

So, are you willing to risk it? Are you better off not praying than risking the humiliation of hearing nothing back? A lot of people think you are.

Common Cause

James was an engineer. He had a good mind and was destined to move up in his company. He also was faithful to Susan, his wife. They attended the community church every Sunday. When Susan wanted to have a daily time of prayer together as husband and wife, however, James opposed it. His scientific mind had not ruled out the existence of God, just his value to everyday life. James didn't think prayer was worth the effort.

James isn't alone. Saul was that way too. He was Jewish and probably more religious than James. James is our contemporary; Saul was the king of Israel in the Old Testament. He was not much of a man of prayer. In fact, he tried praying a couple of times and got burned.

"So Saul asked God, 'Shall I go down after the Philistines? Will you give them into Israel's hand?' But God did not answer him that day" (1 Sam. 14:37). On another occasion Saul "inquired of the LORD, but the LORD did not answer him by dreams or Urim or prophets" (1 Sam. 28:6). As far as I can determine, these were the only times Israel's first king prayed to God. He was a failure both times.

If answered prayer is so exhilarating and unanswered prayer so frustrating, should you risk it? Maybe you ought to leave well enough alone. What defeat could be more devastating than getting your hopes up and then failing to have your prayers answered?

Before you decide you don't want to risk prayer, understand that the most common cause of unanswered prayer is not a silent God—it's our silence, yours and mine. Failure to pray results in a much greater risk of defeat than God's failure to answer. As hockey star Wayne Gretzky said, "You miss one hundred percent of the shots you never take."

Have you ever faced struggle after struggle all day long and then as you lie awake at night, rehearsing your troubles, thought to yourself, "Why didn't I pray about that?" That's happened to me; I suspect it's happened to you. Maybe you shared a prayer request with your church, got the prayer chain cranked up, but forgot to pray yourself. What kept you from praying? Prayer blockers. Sometimes these things are tangible, often they are intangible, but they are always real.

In this book we'll explore a dozen blockers that can hinder your prayers. At the top of the list is prayerlessness. Of the things that keep God from answering your prayers, simply forgetting to pray is the most frequent. James is pretty clear about this. "You do not have, because you do not ask God" (James 4:2).

If prayer is how you talk with God, and if God is the key to meeting your needs, what keeps you from prayer? What are your excuses for failing to talk with God? I've asked this question of hundreds of Christians, and their responses have been remarkably similar. See if your failure to pray is linked to any of these excuses.

Excuse #1: "I Don't Know How to Pray"

For some this is not an excuse; it's a fact. There are people who don't have a clue where to begin in prayer. But that's not true for most of us. We may be unskilled at prayer, but it's not a lack of skill that keeps us from prayer.

Ginger was a new Christian. Her neighbor, Pam, had been having Bible studies with her. One day God broke through Ginger's doubts and gloriously saved her. She had never been to church in her life, so Ginger had to start from scratch. She was a real novice at this Christian living business.

Ginger and Pam began to pray together. Ginger wasn't the expert many of us are. She didn't know any of our "professional" prayer jargon. But her heart was sincere, and she prayed with vigor. It was refreshing. As she grew in the faith some subtle changes began showing up in her prayers. She didn't lose her initial enthusiasm, but her prayers became more substantive, more powerful. She became more skillful in talking with God.

If you're a new Christian, don't feel guilty or embarrassed if you don't know how to pray very well. But don't be satisfied with an entry-level prayer life either. Dig into God's Word. Read some of the great prayers of the Bible, and learn what it means to be empowered to pray.[2] You don't want to become "professional," but you do want to become powerful. Here are a few tips on how to pray if you're new at it.

Pray to God the Father

Sounds pretty elementary, doesn't it? Yet many people who pray fail to pray to God. They pray to nature, to the spirit world, to some higher power. God is not an impersonal force, way out there somewhere. He is a person—a person interested in hearing from you. God told Jeremiah, "Call to me and I will answer you and tell you great and unsearchable things you do not know" (Jer. 33:3). What an invitation! God wants us to talk with him.

In some ways, prayer is like going on a fishing trip. Your buddies and you set out before dawn for your favorite lake. You fish all day, laugh at one another, tell a few hard-to-believe stories, and then go home. Your wife asks, "How'd the day go?" "Great," you reply. "Did you catch anything?" "Not much," you say with a smile.

What made the day so great if you came home without a line of fish? Every fisherman knows the answer. It's not what you catch that makes a fishing trip enjoyable, it's the time you spend with your friends. The same is true with God. Prayer is not a fishing trip, it is valuable time spent with God. If we are praying to a statue, a spirit, or a saint, we're being robbed. When we pray to God, we spend quality time with the Sovereign of the universe.

C. S. Lewis understood this when he wrote, "Prayer in the sense of petition, asking for things, is a small part of it; confession and penitence are its threshold, adoration its sanctuary, the presence and vision and enjoyment of God its bread and wine. In it God shows Himself to us. That He answers prayers is a corollary—not necessarily the most important one—from that revelation. What He does is learned from what He is."[3]

If you're just learning how to pray, start by getting to know the One you pray to. Enjoy your time with him. Be intimate with God when you pray. Prayer isn't reciting words to a distant deity. It's spending enjoyable time with a respected friend.

Pray in Jesus' Name

Have you listened carefully to others as they pray? Likely they said "Amen" at the end of their prayer. That's a term of agreement. It comes from a Hebrew word meaning to support or confirm. In fact, ʾ*amen* is Hebrew for *amen*. Saying amen after someone read the Torah or offered a solemn prayer was a custom that passed from Jewish synagogues into the Christian assemblies of the first century.

You may also have overheard people pray "in Jesus' name." That's a way of praying in Jesus' authority. It means to use the name of Jesus as the key that unlocks the door to

God's throne room. Lehman Strauss illustrates this beauti-
fully in his book *Sense and Nonsense about Prayer*. He says,
"More than once I have been in a strange city and needed to
ask directions. In one sentence, someone might tell me, 'Take
the second road to the right, the fourth to the left, to the traffic signal past the red-brick church, and you can't miss it.'
But I would! However, once I asked directions of a man sitting in a pickup truck at a gas station. He said, 'Follow me;
I'll take you there.' To me, that man was the way, and I did
not miss it!"[4]

That's what praying in Jesus' name is all about. He is the
way. He doesn't tell us how to pray to God, he takes us there.
"In Jesus' name" is not just a tag placed on the end of our
prayers. It's our gateway to God. It's how Jesus takes us there.

Pray in the Holy Spirit

Praying in the Holy Spirit is praying in the power of the
Spirit. Jude 20 says, "But you, dear friends, build yourselves
up in your most holy faith and pray in the Holy Spirit." He's
saying we should grow in God's Word and pray in God's Spirit.

When Paul instructed us to suit up for spiritual warfare, he
followed the checklist of armor with this injunction: "And
pray in the Spirit on all occasions with all kinds of prayers
and requests" (Eph. 6:18). There must be a link between praying in the Spirit and success in spiritual warfare against Satan.

R. Kent Hughes may have had this link in mind when he
wrote:

> When we pray in the Spirit, two supernatural things hap-
> pen to our prayers. First, the Holy Spirit tells us what we
> ought to pray for. Apart from the Holy Spirit's assistance,
> our prayers are limited to our own reason and intuition,
> but with the Holy Spirit's help they move to a higher level.
> . . . The second thing that praying in the Spirit provides is
> the energy of the Holy Spirit for prayer, energizing tired,

even infirm bodies, elevating the depressed to pray with power and conviction for God's work.[5]

If you don't know how to pray, start with these basic principles: pray to the Father, in the name of the Son, and in the power of the Holy Spirit. Once you gain some experience in praying this way, you'll know better how to pray than those who have just stumbled through prayer for years.

Excuse #2: "I Don't Feel Close Enough to God"

If success in prayer depended on how close we are to God, how close would be close enough? The distance between a holy God and sinful people is so great that it cannot be perceptibly calibrated.

When I was a pastor, a woman in my church was on a diet. She had lost five pounds and excitedly announced it to everyone at a party. With typical spousal encouragement, her husband whispered to me, "If you take a cup of water out of Niagara Falls, who notices it?" Sometimes I feel that way about calibrating our closeness to God. When we begin so far away from God, what difference does it make if we take a couple of steps toward him?

Getting "Calvary Close"

We can never be close enough to God to pray without first coming to Jesus Christ as Savior. Without new life in Christ, moving infinitesimally closer to God is like taking a cup of water out of Niagara Falls.

Paul addressed the issue of our closeness in Ephesians 2:12–13:

Remember that at that time you [Gentiles] were separate from Christ, excluded from citizenship in Israel and foreigners to the covenants of the promise, without hope and without God in the world. But now in Christ Jesus you who once were far away have been brought near through the blood of Christ.

While sin separates everyone from God, Gentiles are particularly alienated from him. Gentiles are aliens to God's Messiah, God's nation, God's covenants, God's hope, and God himself. But all that changed one day at a place called Calvary. There Jesus offered his own life as payment for our sin (Eph. 1:7). As a result, we who once were aliens and estranged from God have been made "Calvary close" by the blood of Christ.

Without Christ, you are a kazillion light-years from God. But with Jesus as your Savior, you are reconciled to God and brought near to him (2 Cor. 5:17–18). You can never excuse your failure to pray on not being close to God. Christ made you "Calvary close." Enjoy your proximity.

Moving Away from God

Even after we have been brought close to God by salvation, there are days when our Christian walk appears to take us in the wrong direction. We can't walk out on salvation, but we do seem to be walking out on God. When we aren't as close to God as we should be, that's when it is most difficult to pray.

Ask yourself what former New York City mayor Ed Koch used to ask New Yorkers: "How am I doing?" Do you feel as close to God as you did a few years ago? If you're not enjoying the intimate relationship with God you once did, who moved?

Linda and I began dating in the early '60s. Most of our dates took us to church or Youth for Christ rallies. Afterward all the "cool" kids rendezvoused at The Wolverine, a local drive-in with curb service. My '57 Chevy fit right in.

Linda would sit right next to me in the car. It was like we were joined at the hip. You could have put the Dallas Cowboys' defensive line between her and the passenger door.

Alas, now they could sit in the middle. When she asks why we don't sit as close anymore, I remind her that I didn't move.

If you aren't as close to God as you once were, remember who moved. The trail that leads away from God also leads back. To get your prayer life going again, come back home where you belong.

Prayer as Catalyst

Ironically, those who fail to pray because they don't feel close to God may not feel close to God because they fail to pray. Prayer doesn't move us away from God, but it can be the catalyst to draw us back to him.

E. M. Bounds observed, "Neglect of prayer has always brought loss of faith, loss of love, and loss of prayer. Failure to pray has been the baneful, inevitable cause of backsliding and estrangement from God."[6] If the absence of prayer leads us away from God, what would a return to prayer mean? What if all who complain they aren't close enough to God to pray began to pray? What would happen then?

Excuse #3: "I'm Too Busy to Pray"

Of all the excuses for failing to pray, this is the lamest. Lack of time is never a justifiable reason for not doing something. It's just a flimsy excuse. We each have as much time as everybody else—1,440 minutes each day. We have no less nor more time than those great "prayer warriors" we've heard about. These hours are God's gift to us. What we do with them is our gift to him.

Strangely, this excuse is one that many pastors and Christian leaders use. They cling to it to justify their failure to pray. I believe the primary reason God doesn't place his hand of blessing on a person's ministry is that person's neglect of prayer. When I am weak in prayer, I am weak in everything else as well. As one pastor said, "The principal cause of my leanness and unfruitfulness is owing to an unaccountable backwardness to pray."

Prayer as Ministry

Charles was a busy pastor. He had sermons to prepare, couples to counsel, committee meetings to attend, and hurt feelings to mend. Charles was good at what he did. He genuinely loved his people and sacrificially gave of himself, perhaps giving more than he had to give.

The months and years wore on, and Charles began to feel dry spiritually. As ministry demands on his time grew, his quiet time with God diminished. There was still time for Bible study, of course; he had sermons to prepare. But Charles never seemed to have enough time just to be with God, to enjoy his Word and commune with him in prayer. He was entering the spiritual equivalent of the Twilight Zone.

E. M. Bounds reminds us, "How easily may men, even leaders in Zion, be led by the insidious wiles of Satan to cut short our praying in the interests of the work! How easy to neglect prayer or abbreviate our praying simply by the plea that we have Church work on our hands. Satan has effectively disarmed us when he can keep us too busy doing things to stop and pray."[7]

The fledgling church in Jerusalem had its problems. Peter, John, and the other church leaders were constantly being dragged before the authorities. This church never seemed to be without persecution.

Then a problem of a different kind surfaced within the church. The Grecian Jews complained that insufficient attention was being paid to their widows. An appeal was made to the apostles, and seven Spirit-filled deacons were selected to care for the needs of these widows. Why were deacons needed for this task? What were the spiritual leaders doing?

"We . . . will give our attention to prayer and the ministry of the word" (Acts 6:3–4).

The most efficient use of a pastor's time in the local church is in the ministry of prayer and the preaching of the Word. It's strange, isn't it, that these apostles neglected to mention the obligatory committee meetings, the hours of counseling, and that nasty plumbing job in the church basement. They clearly understood the chief ministries of church leadership to be prayer and the Word, in that order.

Satan easily deludes us into thinking that activity is the same as spirituality. This is never true. As the old hymn says, "Take time to be holy, the world rushes on; Spend much time in secret with Jesus alone." When we are in love with someone, one of the proofs of that love is our desire to spend time with him or her. Could it be that our failure to spend time with God is speaking volumes about our love for him?

If you aren't hearing from God, perhaps it's because he isn't hearing from you. Carve out some time each day for your appointment with him. Don't let anyone or anything infringe on that time. Make time for God!

Excuse #4: "It Doesn't Work Anyway"

Wendy was a young mother. Little Justin, her two-year-old, kept her hopping. As a single mom, she lived a pretty harried life. Wendy not only had to tend to her own needs, but she had to get Justin up, dressed, and off to day care each morning before she went to work.

Wendy knew she had to provide for Justin and herself, but she also wanted to get better acquainted with God. She set her alarm for 5:30 each morning just to have a quiet time. She felt pretty good about her relationship with God.

Then one day Wendy received a call from the day care. Something was wrong with Justin. The voice on the phone said, "Go to the County General emergency room right away." The day care director had called 911 because Justin was having severe seizures. Wendy thought, "I prayed this morning that God would take care of Justin, and now this. What's the use of praying?"

Sound familiar? We've all been there. Perhaps the most frequent reason why people fail to pray is because they just don't believe it works.

I Need Real Answers

When we need answers to our prayers, we need real answers, not platitudes from our friends. It's true that "all things work together for good" (see Rom. 8:28), but it's just as true that it's hard to hang in there while things are working out.

Harold Lindsell comments, "Mrs. Jonathan Goforth wrote an entire book that had for its theme, 'How I Know God Answers Prayer.' Puzzling questions enter the minds of thoughtful people at this point, questions that can quickly cause one to sink into a labyrinth of confusion. Were the so-called answers to prayer really answers? Would not the same things have occurred if there had been no prayer?"[8] Ever ask yourself these questions? Inquiring minds want to know if prayer really works. Yet we can't say prayer *doesn't* work. Too many people have experienced answers to their prayers.

Prayer is perhaps the greatest weapon in the Christian's arsenal against Satan. The last thing the devil wants is for us to believe in the power of prayer. As long as he can make us think that prayer doesn't work, we won't use it, and Satan wins.

Where's the Evidence?

Can we dismiss prayer the way we dismiss fairy tales? No. The evidence is there, but our skeptical minds prefer to see changed events as twists of fate rather than answers to prayer. As long as that's true, we will never find evidence that God has answered our prayers. Lindsell says,

> If anyone asks for incontrovertible evidence to validate the efficacy of prayer beyond all question of doubt, it is impossible to produce it. It would be equally impossible to do so in any other realm of life. But if we are willing to consider credible reports seriously and to come to conclusions based on the same kind of evidences such as we employ to arrive at conclusions in other areas of life, the power of prayer may be demonstrated to the satisfaction of reasonable men.[9]

Does prayer work? Ask a skeptic, and you'll get a skeptic's response. Ask someone who believes in prayer, and you'll get a different response. Some day, ask King Hezekiah (2 Kings 19:14–35). Ask King Jehoshaphat (2 Chron. 20:1–25). Ask Daniel (Dan. 6:10–22). Ask Jesus (Matt. 7:7–11). They all believed that God answers prayer. Ask your godly grandmother. Ask that simple country church deacon. Ask anyone who has received an answer from God. They all believe God answers prayer. There must be good reason.

What's a Person to Do?

At the bottom line, whether or not you believe in answered prayer largely depends on your faith in sources. If you trust the person who claims God answers prayer, you will trust that prayer was answered. Too many people have experienced the power of answered prayer for it to be dismissed as improbable. Jesus believed in prayer or he wouldn't have spent so much time praying. If you have trusted him as your Savior, shouldn't you trust what he says about God's ability to answer prayer?

If God doesn't seem to be paying attention to you, investigate how much you're paying attention to him. The most frequent cause for unanswered prayer is our failure to pray. Prayerlessness is a major prayer blocker.

Commit the big and little details of your life to God. Believe he will answer when you pray. Put your spiritual antennae up to receive that answer. Heed the words of Joseph Scriven's beloved hymn: "Oh what peace we often forfeit, oh what needless pain we bear, all because we do not carry everything to God in prayer."

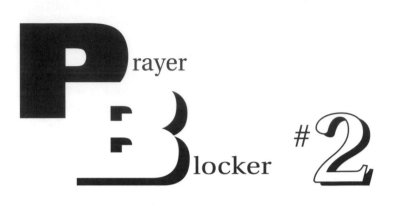

Prayer Blocker #2

God doesn't answer when

We Cherish Sin

> We are too Christian really to enjoy sinning, and too fond of sinning really to enjoy Christianity. Most of us know perfectly well what we ought to do; our trouble is that we do not want to do it.
>
> Peter Marshall

I have to begin this chapter with an admission of guilt. I'm a recovering chocoholic. Actually, that's not entirely true. I am a chocoholic, but I'm not recovering. I love chocolate.

Hershey. Cadbury. Godiva. Ghirardelli. These are my heroes—dear friends, not just distant acquaintances. I never met a piece of chocolate I didn't like.

Add to this that I also love ice cream (one of the four basic food groups), and you have a divine combination—ice cream and chocolate. Throw in a few friends and voilà—the chocolate sundae.

Begin with three scoops of ice cream. (You may use vanilla if you wish, but why would you when there is double Dutch chocolate, chocolate almond, and chocolate fudge?) Place them in a dish. Cover them with a generous portion of chocolate syrup, then whipped cream, some nuts, a little more chocolate syrup, and a cherry on top.

There are variations on this theme, of course, but the melody that emanates from a chocolate sundae is like music to my ears. It's a symphony to the salivary glands. Some say it's delightfully sinful.

This leads us into a second observation about why God sometimes doesn't answer prayer. Whatever is delightfully sinful is also deadly to our prayer life—not chocolate sundaes necessarily, but anything we delight in that's wrong. Sin deals a major blow to getting answers to our prayers. It's a rock-hard prayer blocker.

One of the psalmists (probably David) wrote a song for the director of music in the tabernacle. Psalm 66 is an uplifting and exciting call to praise God: "Shout with joy to God, all the earth! Sing the glory of his name; make his praise glorious! Say to God, 'How awesome are your deeds!'" (Ps. 66:1–3).

Again and again the psalmist invites us to investigate the goodness of God: "Come and see what God has done, how awesome his works in man's behalf!" (v. 5). "Come and listen, all you who fear God; let me tell you what he has done for me" (v. 16).

Here's a man with confidence in God. He believed that when he prayed, God listened. In fact he said clearly, "God has surely listened and heard my voice in prayer. Praise be to God, who has not rejected my prayer or withheld his love from me!" (vv. 19–20).

It's fulfilling, isn't it, when we are able to be that confident. How exhilarating to know that God listened to me and heard my prayer. He didn't reject what I said but granted my requests instead. No one in his right mind would not want that.

Hearts That Hide Sin

God does not always listen when we pray, however, and the psalmist knew why. There's a fly in the ointment of prayer. God has established some conditions to hearing us and answering our prayers. One is as plain as day: "If I had cherished sin in my heart, the Lord would not have listened" (Ps. 66:18).

There's the bombshell. The psalmist knew that if he delighted in what was sinful, while at the same time praying to God, God would not listen to his prayer. God simply pays no attention to us when we harbor sin in our lives and act as if it weren't there.

What does the psalmist mean when he speaks of "cherishing" sin in our hearts? The Hebrew word *(rasah)* means to approve or enjoy, to show respect to something.

That's not too difficult to understand. If we are enjoying sin and praying to God at the same time, we are showing more respect to sin than to God. God is under no obligation to listen to prayers that come from disrespectful hearts. If we approve of something we know is wrong and attempt to talk with God at the same time, we might as well save our breath.

Suppose you work in an office where you enter data into a computer. You've worked for your company almost ten years and are a model employee. You're never late to work, you never purloin paper clips, you don't even stretch your fifteen-minute coffee break to twenty minutes. You're the kind of person the boss likes to have around.

However, you've developed a juicy little habit over the years. You're attractive, and you like to flirt a little with the men in your office. Nothing serious, just a little tease here and there. You would never let it get out of hand. You love your husband and your children, and they love you. It's just something you like to do.

But as the months pass, you find yourself attracted to one guy at the office a little more than you should be. At first you denied it, but you can't any longer. You've flirted with him regularly, and now you think he's beginning to show some interest in you.

What do you do? Maybe you pray, "Lord, you know how I am. I like to flirt a little. But Lord, this is getting serious. I beg of you, please don't let this relationship develop into anything that would hurt my family. All I want to do is have a little fun."

You're doing exactly what the psalmist said you cannot do if you want God to answer your prayers. You cannot cherish sin and have God protect you from it at the same time. Asking God to keep you from future sin without owning up to present sin is like asking the bank to loan you money to pay debts you can't handle now.

The blessings the psalmist praised God for in Psalm 66 came because he had dealt with his personal sin. He did not regard iniquity in his heart, and therefore God was pleased to hear his prayer and bless him.

If you want God to answer your prayers, check the things you cherish. Unless you come clean with God, you are wasting your time when you pray. God does not listen to lips that hide sin in the heart.

Sin Dulls Hearing

Linda and I were married while I was in college. Actually I had graduated from one college and was enrolled in a second one taking a different major before I went to seminary and graduate school. We were married between my first college graduation and the second.

That year we moved to a distant city where we found a two-room apartment. It was really tiny—just a bedroom and living room with an adjoining bath. We rented it from an elderly lady who lived downstairs. Linda and I shared her kitchen, her refrigerator (she had two shelves and we had two shelves), and her telephone.

She was a delightful old gal but dreadfully hard of hearing. Without her two hearing aids, she was almost deaf. Occasionally we would surprise her in the morning before she had them in her ears. Until she saw you, no amount of noise could get her attention.

Because of her severe auditory impairment, our landlady had the telephone company replace the bells on her phone with two four-inch bells. That increased their volume to something like the bells of the Notre Dame cathedral. When the phone rang at night, we would be a foot off the bed before we realized what the noise was.

When I pray and God doesn't seem to be listening, I always remember that lady. No matter how loudly I talked with her, she couldn't hear a word until her hearing aids were turned on. I was wasting my breath. It was useless.

The Divine Ear

Have you ever wondered if God was hard of hearing? Why does he not respond to your prayers? Is he, like my college landlady, severely hearing impaired?

Not in the least. The divine ear is not dull. The prophet Isaiah knew that. He said, "Surely the arm of the LORD is not too short to save, nor his ear too dull to hear" (Isa. 59:1).

The prophet was speaking anthropomorphically of God. He described God as you would a man. God's arm was not too short to save. No one is beyond his grasp. His arm is long enough to reach the most distant sinner. We can never blame our spiritual failures on the limits of God's ability.

The same is true when it comes to answering prayer. We can never blame the failure of our prayers on the divine ear. When he chooses to listen, God has no difficulty hearing us. We can be sure that when God does not hear our prayers, it's more often than not because of something in our life that keeps him from listening.

A Defective Uplink

The problem in getting answers from God is our sin, not his hearing. Isaiah said, "Your iniquities have separated you from your God; your sins have hidden his face from you" (Isa. 59:2).

When our prayer link to heaven is severed, it's not because there's something wrong with the downlink. The trouble is with the uplink. Our sin blocks the connection we have with God. When we deal with our sin, we deal with the source of interference on the line. Confessing sin is like reconnecting the satellite uplink.

Are you experiencing some difficulty in getting answers to your prayers? Don't assume sin is always the problem, but don't underestimate the power of sin. When you pray and delight in some sin at the same time, God is neither impressed nor inclined to answer. He is not impressed with a heart that would seek him in prayer without surrendering sin in order to pray successfully. God is not inclined to answer the prayer of someone who shows so little regard for his holiness.

Problems and Promises

Suppose we had no lines of communication open to God. What would it be like if we could never get through to him? Maybe it would be like hitting the redial button on the telephone after we had failed to reach someone. Our failure is repeated again and again.

Millions of people experience that feeling every day. They cherish their sin and won't let go of it. They carry around sin's penalty because they have never asked Jesus Christ to save them. Until they do, they have no relationship that will allow them to speak with God.

A Problem for Some

This becomes a real problem for some people. Their personal sin prevents a connection every time they try to pray to God. Not just some times—every time. They can't get through because they don't have the kind of relationship with God that permits them to get through.

The Bible speaks to this problem in many places. Solomon mentions it twice in one chapter. In Proverbs 15:8 he says, "The LORD detests the sacrifice of the wicked, but the prayer of the upright pleases him." For people who want God to hear them on their own terms, that's not good news. Even if they bring a sacrifice to God in order to bribe him when they pray, God sees right through it.

Even more to the point is what Solomon says in verse 29 of Proverbs 15: "The LORD is far from the wicked but he hears the prayer of the righteous." It's not that God isn't listening to the prayers of those who are still in rebellion against him, it's much worse. God is actually distancing himself from them. They are far from him—out of earshot. When they pray it's like whistling in the wind. Their prayers are empty, hollow, and ineffective because they cherish sin more than they cherish God.

A Promise to Others

Just the opposite is true for those who have found a relationship with God through Jesus Christ. Not only are we in a position to be heard by God, but he actually delights in hearing from us.

Remember the second half of Proverbs 15:8: "the prayer of the upright pleases him." God finds detestable the sacrifice of those who live in disregard for him, but he is pleased to hear the prayers of those who live in harmony with him. That's quite a contrast.

Part two of Proverbs 15:29 is equally striking. Although God is far from the wicked, "he hears the prayer of the righteous." God's promise to you is that if you live righteously, you are on the fast track to getting your prayers answered.

If you have never asked Jesus Christ to be your Savior, you cannot live righteously before God. It's impossible, for we are all sinners, stained with sin and plagued with sin's consequences (see Rom. 3:10, 23; 6:23). But when you have faith that Jesus died to pay the penalty for your sin (see 2 Cor. 5:21), you take him to be your righteousness. That's when the uplink to God is opened for the first time. Trusting Jesus as Savior is the first step in getting your prayers answered.

The Secret Room

Even if you have taken this first step, it's still possible to cherish sin in your life. There may be a hidden room in your mind or in your heart that you don't want to give up. You say to Jesus, "Thanks for dying for me and saving me. I'll give you everything in my life—everything, that is, except this one secret room. That I want to keep for myself."

Many Christians have such a secret room. In it they keep that one sin that haunts them, that one sin they enjoy so much they just can't walk away from it. Maybe you have such a room. In the dark recesses of your heart you cherish something so wicked that you would just die if anybody knew about it.

Remember my love of chocolate sundaes? Suppose I slipped into the kitchen alone, late at night, night after night, to cherish a secret chocolate sundae? Do you think my wife would know? Would she ever discover that I wasn't in bed for a half hour, night after night? And what about my weight? Do you think my middle-of-the-night rendezvous with seven hundred calories would adversely affect my weight? I might think I'm hiding my cherished secret, but in reality I'd only be fooling myself.

The same is true with praying while we secretly enjoy some ongoing sin. Secret sins, cherished sins, have a devastating effect on our prayer life. Maybe we can hide them for a while, but eventually they always reveal themselves.

When you or I cherish sin in this way—any sin—we can remove the pronoun *I* from Psalm 66:18 and write our name in its place. We may be keeping a sin or two because we treasure them, but they are keeping our prayers from being heard and answered by God.

What's a Person to Do?

If you don't feel God is listening to you when you pray, or if it appears he is not answering you, there are some dos and don'ts to keep in mind.

Don't stop praying. Prayer is the vehicle to convey your innermost desires to God. There's nothing wrong with the vehicle. Don't throw up your hands and say, "Prayer doesn't work. I'm wasting my time." Prayer does work, but you may have other problems.

Don't blame God for not answering your prayers. God has more than enough power to answer every prayer that pleases him, from every person who pleases him. His power is not the issue; pleasing him is.

Do be introspective. Look inside yourself. See what God sees there and be truthful about it. You have nothing to lose and everything to gain. Ask yourself, "Is it possible I am the problem? Is there something I'm trying to hide from God that's blocking my way to him?" These are serious questions, but they never are asked by people who continually fail to get answers to their prayers.

Do be honest with God. When you identify what it is that displeases him, don't try to cover it up. "He who conceals his sins does not prosper, but whoever confesses and renounces them finds mercy" (Prov. 28:13). Remember, you can't hide your sin from God anyway. "He reveals deep and hidden things; he knows what lies in darkness" (Dan. 2:22; cf. Deut. 29:29; Luke 8:17; Heb. 4:13).

Do be honest with yourself. Cherished sin is a prayer blocker of the worst kind. Something has to be done about unconfessed sin if you are to have a clear shot at getting your prayers answered. The only thing that works is confession and repentance—openly and honestly tell God what you know is keeping your prayers from being answered and ask his forgiveness.

Here's the good news: "If we confess our sins, he is faithful and just and will forgive us our sins and purify us from all unrighteousness" (1 John 1:9). Sin is a prayer blocker; honest confession of sin is dynamite. When you apply dynamite to a prayer blocker, the explosion is heard all the way to heaven.

You can get answers to your prayers. Remove the blocker of hidden, unconfessed, cherished sin and pave the way for God to hear and answer your prayers.

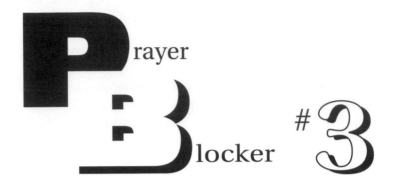

Prayer Blocker #3

God doesn't answer when

We Have a Faulty Relationship with God

> Whoever only speaks of God, but never or seldom to God,
> easily leases body and soul to idols.
> Carl F. H. Henry

Why did God create humankind? Why did God, who needs nothing, bring you and me into this world? It wasn't because he was lonely. God the Father, God the Son, and God the Spirit have perfect harmony and fellowship with each other. You and I have little to contribute to divine fellowship. So why did he create us? I believe it was so we could share in the benefits of having a relationship with him. God created us to glorify him and in so doing to enjoy a relationship with him.

Our first parents enjoyed such a relationship. God walked and talked with Adam and Eve. But when they sinned, they put a crimp in that beautiful relationship with God. As a result, our relationship with God has been faulty ever since. It is only when that relationship is repaired through faith in Jesus Christ that we can truly glorify God as we were created to do.

But the damage done by sin to our vital relationship with God affects much more than just our walk with him. It also affects our talk with him. Because sin erects relational roadblocks between God and us, these roadblocks keep us from getting through to God. When we fail to treat God as he deserves, our communication with God is one of the first casualties of that failure.

What are some of the failures that keep our prayers from being effective? The Bible identifies many of them, but three that relate directly to God seem to surface regularly:

1. failure to respect God
2. failure to abide in Christ
3. failure to heed God's Word

Are you having trouble getting answers to your prayers? If so, examine your relationship with God in these three areas. If you find your relationship is inadequate, you may have hit on the cause for unanswered prayer in your life.

Failure to Respect God

We all know who God is. He's the Creator, the Sustainer, the Sovereign God. He's the eternal, omniscient, loving Redeemer of mankind. But when we say all that, it sounds as though what we know about God comes right out of a textbook. Who is God, really? Reach down deep into your daily experience and identify who God is in your life.

It's one thing to expound the virtues of God as if you just came out of Theology 101 class. It's quite another to see God through the piles of dirty laundry or the mundane sameness of data entry.

What is your relationship with God? How do you treat him? If you say you respect him, would he know it from the attitudes and actions of your life today? If you examined everything in your life for the fingerprints of God, would there be sufficient evidence to prove you have a vibrant relationship with him?

These are tough questions, and you may find them difficult to answer. Sometimes we allow sin to creep into our lives; that's when our relationship with God is truly tested. It's also when we wonder if he is listening to our prayers.

We are not the first to experience this. The Jews of the Old Testament had the same problem. Every time Israel caved in to idolatry, they had difficulty getting their prayers answered.

God sent prophet after prophet to warn the Jewish people about their faulty relationship with him. The list reads like a Who's Who of the Old Testament.

Ezekiel's Warning

Ezekiel was a captive in Babylon. The Jews were exiled there as punishment for their idolatry. From his house along the Kebar River, Ezekiel was taken by a vision to Jerusalem (Ezek. 8). There God showed him the pagan idols and the detestable things that were going on in his sanctuary.

It was then God made this startling statement: "Therefore I will deal with them in anger; I will not look on them with pity or spare them. Although they shout in my ears, I will not listen to them" (Ezek. 8:18). Imagine. God told his chosen people that because they had treated him poorly, he wouldn't listen to them. They could shout right in his ears; it wouldn't matter.

God hates nothing more than idolatry. When people, even God's people, give their love and allegiance to anyone or anything other than God, he refuses to hear their prayers. That's how deeply a faulty relationship with God affects our ability to get through to him.

Micah's Warning

Enter the prophet Micah. He had the same message for Judah. Because God's people had embraced false prophets, which is a form of idolatry, Micah said, "Then they will cry out to the LORD, but he will not answer them. At that time he will hide his face from them because of the evil they have done" (Micah 3:4).

Micah used an even stronger word than did Ezekiel for crying unto God. His verb means to shriek. Even if the Jews shrieked to God, if they prayed in loud and boisterous terms, that still would be insufficient reason for God to answer them. In fact, God promised to conceal his face from his people because of their idolatry.

Why? Because they had been disrespectful to God. They placed more value on idols than they did in God. Their faulty relationship with God destroyed their ability to pray in a meaningful and successful way.

Zechariah's Warning

For Zechariah it was the same story. He began his prophecy with these words: "The LORD was very angry with your fore-fathers. Therefore tell the people: This is what the LORD Almighty says: 'Return to me,' declares the LORD Almighty, 'and I will return to you'" (Zech. 1:2–3).

Talk about starting off with a bang. This is high drama. Jewish idolatry had alienated the people from God. Their relationship had become faulty, and their respect for Jehovah had fallen to an all-time low.

How did God respond to the idolatry of the Jews? He said to Zechariah, "'When I called, they did not listen; so when they called, I would not listen,' says the LORD Almighty" (Zech. 7:13).

Don't get the idea that Jehovah is a pouting God, sitting in heaven playing tit for tat. God's refusal to hear the prayers of his people was divine judgment, not divine sulking.

When we treat God poorly, when we are guilty of any form of idolatry, why do we expect him to answer our prayers? Why should he? A faulty relationship with God dramatically impacts his willingness to answer when we pray.

Jeremiah's Warning

Then there was Jeremiah. Three times he was told to warn God's people that their idolatry kept them from getting answers to their prayers.

In Jeremiah 7:16 God said, "So do not pray for this people nor offer any plea or petition for them; do not plead with me, for I will not listen to you." Sounds pretty harsh, doesn't it?

Again in Jeremiah 11:14 he said, "Do not pray for this people nor offer any plea or petition for them, because I will not listen when they call to me in the time of their distress." Think about it. God says he will not even listen, let alone answer.

Once more, this time in Jeremiah 14:12, God said, "Although they fast, I will not listen to their cry; though they offer burnt offerings and grain offerings, I will not accept them. Instead, I will destroy them with the sword, famine and plague."

At this point you may be saying, "I had no idea verses like these were in the Bible. I thought God always heard our prayers, even if he didn't answer them." Well, read again.

God's anger at idolatry was so fierce that he refused to hear the Jews' prayers just as he refused to accept their offerings. They had treated God poorly. What he was looking for was their repentance. Until that came, there was no use talking to him.

Idolatry Today

Are we any different today? Not much. Often we are just as idolatrous as Israel was. We may not fall face down before an idol of stone and treat it with the respect due only to God, but we have the same penchant for idolatry. We'll pay forty dollars for a ticket to a football game and then gripe about putting five dollars in the offering plate at church. Isn't that cherishing football more than we cherish God? That's idolatry.

When do you take your break from housework in the afternoon? Is it at just the right time to watch the soaps or the talk shows? Do you then rationalize that you don't have time to prepare a Sunday school lesson so you can't be a teacher? Isn't that cherishing Oprah or Geraldo more than God? That's idolatry. If you can easily justify buying a new microwave, a new car, or a new VCR but have trouble meeting your pledge to the missions budget at church, haven't you fallen into a form of idolatry?

Can you see why your prayers may sometimes be ignored by God? If something is stealing the quality of your relationship with God, until that relationship is repaired, the chances of God hearing your prayers are greatly diminished.

Are you treating God well enough for him to answer your prayers? A faulty relationship with God will keep him from hearing you just as he refused to hear Israel. The next time you pray, ask yourself this question first: "If I were God and was treated the way I've treated him today, would I be inclined to answer my own prayers?" If you haven't been treating God with the respect he deserves, start there. Treat him as if he were the eternal, omniscient, loving Redeemer of mankind. After all, he is.

If you're not getting answers to your prayers, check your relationship with God. If you've been a bit idolatrous lately, putting other things or other people ahead of God, why are you surprised when he doesn't answer? Right your relationship with God. Begin to treat him as a supreme being ought to be treated. Then watch your prayer potency grow. How you treat God affects how he answers your prayers.

Failure to Abide in Christ

God has revealed himself to us in several ways. The two most prominent are through his Son, Jesus Christ—the Living Word—and through the Bible—the written Word. Sometimes a ruptured relationship with God most quickly shows up in how we treat his Son or his Word.

Let's investigate how faulty relationships here can negatively impact getting answers to our prayers.

Nearly two thousand years ago, when Jesus walked the dusty roads of Galilee and Judea, he healed the sick, gave sight to the blind, raised the dead, and did many other wonderful things that proved he was God. The words that Jesus spoke and the things that he did were not his own. Jesus did not speak his own mind; he spoke the things that were on his Father's mind. Jesus did not do his own will; he did only his Father's will. Jesus was completely obedient to his Father.

The relationship between God the Father and God the Son was never a faulty one. They respected each other. They had unbroken communication, except for those hours on the cross (see Matt. 27:46). Jesus knew that God the Father always heard him when he prayed (John 11:41). He had no trouble getting answers to his prayers.

If Jesus had God's ear, why does it sometimes seem that God isn't listening to us? Perhaps we fail to maintain the relationship with him that his Son did. Perhaps we fail to maintain the relationship with his Son that the Father did. But how do we maintain that relationship?

Shelter and Shadow

Some people only run to Christ when they are in trouble. You know the kind. They want to enjoy the ultimate fruit of salvation—eternity in heaven—but for now they want to live life as they please. They don't want to remain in Jesus twenty-four hours a day. They want him only when they need him. They want to be Sunday-morning Christians.

Remember what the psalmist said in Psalm 91? "He who dwells in the shelter of the Most High will rest in the shadow of the Almighty." If we want to enjoy the shelter of the Most High and the protection of the shadow of the Almighty, we cannot run to him only when we are in trouble. We must have the mature discipline to live in him, to sojourn with him, to throw our lot in with him.

Our relationship with the Son of God will be faulty as long as we think of it as an on-demand relationship. When it helps us, when it meets our needs, we want it. But when we have to put something into it, we'd rather not be bothered. It's ours on demand.

How do you treat Jesus? As a big brother who will bail you out when others pick on you? Or do you express your love and respect for him by hanging out with him throughout the day and night? Is he your constant shelter and shadow? Your relationship with him is the most important relationship you have. Make sure it's a good one.

A Prayer Life on the Fritz

What if we want to live our own way and only go to Jesus when we need him? What if we have little interest in his words penetrating our mind and providing direction for our life?

These are fair questions. Shall we speculate at the answer? When we fail to abide in Christ, we fail to meet one important criterion for getting answers to our prayers. Jesus said, "If you remain in me and my words remain in you, ask whatever you wish, and it will be given you" (John 15:7). If we want God to hear us when we pray, we must take seriously what Jesus said. Don't run to Jesus; live in him.

Fritz came to America to enroll in seminary. I'll never forget him. His thick German accent gave him an air of dignity and intelligence. Fritz was very bright; it was hard for the rest of us to keep up with him in class.

But Fritz was used to his freedom. I'm sure he loved the Lord, but he also loved to do things his way. "Stubborn German will," Fritz used to say with a twinkle of pride. At first I thought his self-sufficiency was just his personality. After a few months in class with Fritz, however, I could easily detect that he was in the habit of praying to the Lord only when he thought he needed him, and given Fritz's abilities and intellect, that wasn't very often.

Fritz was not abiding in Christ. He was not in the Word daily. Then I discovered that Fritz didn't attend church. He used prayer as a crutch; when Fritz couldn't do it, he trusted that the Lord could. Fritz's prayer life was in shambles because he never learned the secret of constantly abiding in Christ.

It's obvious that getting answers to our prayers is closely linked to how we treat God the Father and God the Son. Before you pray today, maybe you should take a few minutes to reflect on your relationship with God. Maybe you're not as ready to pray as you thought.

Failure to Heed God's Word

Let your mind wander a minute. Suppose you worked in a research lab tracking down cures for dreaded diseases. Your work specialized in nutrition and the effects of various foods on personal health. Day after day you conducted very sophisticated experiments, and day after day you were frustrated by your lack of progress.

Then something wonderful happened. While you were at home lying in your hammock and sipping a glass of lemonade, you noticed that these minutes were the most refreshing, most relaxing, most rejuvenating of your day. You began to wonder if there was any link between your hammock and your good health.

When you returned to the laboratory, it dawned on you: The secret was not the hammock; it was the lemon. You began testing the effects of pure lemon juice on various diseases. Eureka! Almost accidentally you discovered that some properties in fresh-squeezed lemons slowed a rapid pulse rate, lowered cholesterol, broke down the fats in the diet, and could possibly extend life by a dozen years.

This is a hypothetical case, of course, and I'm not suggesting that lemon juice can do any of these things. But suppose it were true. Suppose you found the secret to retarding many disabling conditions in the human body.

You immediately wrote a book about your findings. It had the potential of changing life as we know it on our planet. The book was translated into dozens of languages, printed, and shipped to bookstores around the world. Sales were brisk. People everywhere bought it.

Then something unexplainable happened. People bought your book, but they didn't read it. You made a major discovery that would both extend human life for many years and improve its quality, but nobody paid any attention to what you had to say. You were dumbfounded. What's more, you were heartbroken.

God's Best-Seller

Had this lemon scenario been true, perhaps you would know something of the heartache God must experience. He carefully communicated a message that would save men and women from the devastation of hell and enable them to enjoy his company forever. He communicated it to some forty authors over more than fifteen hundred years. He inspired them in such a way that what they wrote accurately reflected what he revealed. He gave us his written Word—the Holy Bible.

And we bought it. Did we ever buy it. We bought black ones, red ones, burgundy ones, and denim ones. Brides bought white ones to carry down the aisle. Parents bought their children Bibles with cartoons and pictures. Teens bought their own special editions. When we got older, some entrepreneurial publisher even printed giant print editions for those of us with failing eyesight.

United States presidents placed their hand on God's Word when they took the oath of office. Courtroom witnesses did the same to certify that they would tell nothing but the truth. The Bible really got around.

We bought Bibles in such quantities that it became the best-seller of all time. God must have been pleased. So many people were so interested in what he had to say.

But the Bible is a little like exercise bikes. A lot of people buy them, but few people use them. Exercise bikes show up in garage sales more often than anything else. Why? The spirit is willing but the flesh is weak (literally). The same is true with Bibles.

While the number of Bibles printed and purchased is phenomenal, the number of Bibles read and heeded is pitiful. For many people the Bible has become a family heirloom, a coffee table dust gatherer, or the object of a maddening search on Sunday morning that makes you late for church.

I have often said that if everybody blew the dust off their Bibles at the same time, we'd all be killed in the dust storm. We have plenty of questions and the Bible has the answers, but we know so very little about the Bible that our questions largely go unanswered.

Faulty Prayer Life

God is very pointed about how failure to heed his Word affects our prayer life, as well as our personal life. The Book of Proverbs is a collection of moralistic sayings written for the most part by King Solomon, the wisest man who ever lived.

One of those pointed observations is this: "If anyone turns a deaf ear to the law, even his prayers are detestable" (Prov. 28:9).

Just a few pages earlier we thought about God turning a deaf ear to our prayers because we cherished sin in our hearts. Here the wise man turns the tables. If we turn a deaf ear to God and his Word, God finds our prayers "detestable." The word means something that is morally disgusting or abominable to God.

Imagine. The Bible says if we do not pay attention to God's law, that is, his Word, God will find our prayers distasteful, something to be avoided and detested. Should that say something to us about how we treat the Bible?

Dig for Gold

Psalm 19:10 says of the words of God, "They are more precious than gold, than much pure gold; they are sweeter than honey, than honey from the comb." Here's the bottom line. God's Word is to be more precious to us than gold. Since the Bible reveals what's on God's mind, and since it and it alone reveals God's way to heaven, God anticipates that we will want to read his Word, enjoy it, profit from it, memorize it, live by it, and desire it more than we desire much pure gold.

If you knew there was gold buried in your backyard, would you continue reading this book, or would you drop it immediately and go out to dig? Be honest. In fact, if I knew there was gold buried in your backyard, I'd be there in a flash myself.

We have no difficulty mustering the desire to dig for gold. God's Word should be more precious to us than fine gold, and yet sometimes we show so little interest in it that our prayers suffer as a result. We do not treat the Bible well enough for God to answer our prayers.

As an author of dozens of books, the greatest compliment you can pay me is to say you've read my books. You don't necessarily have to say you enjoyed them; reading them is enough for most authors.

May I remind you that God wrote a book—only one book. It's the Bible. I wonder what you'll say to him should he ask you at the judgment seat of Christ, "Did you read my book?" What will you say? How well are you treating God's Word?

What's a Person to Do?

Much of your success in prayer relates to whether you respect God. Do you make time for him? Do you honor him above all else? If you want God to answer your prayers, show him the respect he deserves. Place him first in your life.

You must also cultivate a relationship with Christ. In John 15 Jesus used the metaphor of a vine and its branches to teach his disciples about the importance of a vital relationship with him. He said, "I am the vine; you are the branches. If a man remains in me and I in him, he will bear much fruit; apart from me you can do nothing" (John 15:5). That's the ultimate expression of relationship. Do you know what Jesus meant when he spoke of remaining in him? He taught his disciples that they had to come to him and tarry there. That's what the Greek word *meno* means. Sojourn. Take up residence. Live in Christ's presence and resurrection power. That's abiding in Christ.

Having a right relationship with Christ is vital to your prayer life. Remember Jesus' words in John 15:7: "If you remain in me and my words remain in you, ask whatever you wish, and it will be given you." If you abide in him and make sure his words abide in you, you have the inside track on getting your prayers answered. It all hinges on your relationship with him.

Not only are you to abide in Christ, you are to remain constantly in the Word. If you want God to answer your prayers, show his Word the respect it deserves. Spend enough time in it to make notes of what you read. Marinate your mind in it.

Memorize it. And most of all, obey it. Joshua 1:8 reminds us, "Do not let this Book of the Law depart from your mouth; meditate on it day and night, so that you may be careful to do everything written in it. Then you will be prosperous and successful." If your prayers don't seem to be getting through to God, maybe it's because his Word isn't getting through to you.

Develop a daily relationship with God through his Son and through his Word, and watch your prayer life take a quantum leap forward.

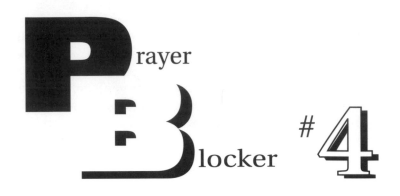

Prayer **B**locker # **4**

God doesn't answer when

We Have Faulty Relationships with Others

> We must alter our lives in order to alter our hearts, for it is impossible to live one way and pray another.
>
> William Law

This is the day of the dysfunctional family. Pick up any newspaper or magazine and you read about it. Books abound on the subject. Radio and television programs have been spawned to help us bring some sense to our relationships with others.

We human beings were created in the image of God. Among other things that means we are relational beings, because God is a relational being. The fact that we speak of God as Father, Son, and Holy Spirit shows that the persons of the Godhead relate to one another. "In the beginning was the Word, and the Word was with God, and the Word was God" (John 1:1). That's relationship. The relationship between the persons of the Godhead is perfect. There is no dysfunction, no disagreements, no arguments, no disputes. There is nothing but perfect harmony.

So how did we who are created in God's image become so dysfunctional? When our first parents, Adam and Eve, disobeyed God in the Garden of Eden, sin entered the human realm and permeated the human family. Since that time, our relationship with God and with others has been on the blink; it has been faulty.

Faulty relationships with others cause hard feelings. We've all experienced that. Faulty relationships also cause mistrust. Perhaps you know that feeling too. But you may not be aware that faulty relationships with others also limit the effectiveness of your prayers.

The High Cost of Not Getting Along

Can failing to live charitably with others be a deterrent to God answering our prayers? At first we may be tempted to say no way. But let's read the words of Jesus: "You have heard that it was said to the people long ago, 'Do not murder, and anyone who murders will be subject to judgment.' But I tell you that anyone who is angry with his brother will be subject to judgment" (Matt. 5:21–22). Here Jesus is talking about the deadly effects of anger. What does it have to do with answered prayer?

Anger can be a real inflammation in life. In his autobiography, humbly entitled *Number One*,[10] the late New York Yankees' manager, Billy Martin, told of an incident when his anger got the best of him. He was hunting with slugger Mickey Mantle on a ranch in south Texas owned by Mantle's friend. When the pair arrived at the gate, Mickey told Martin to stay in the car while he checked in with his friend.

The rancher told Mantle it was okay to hunt but asked a favor of him first. He had an old mule in the barn that was going blind, and he simply didn't have the heart to shoot it.

He asked Mantle if he would do it for him. Mantle agreed, but when he returned to the car, he pretended to be angry and told Billy Martin, "That guy won't let us hunt. I'm so mad that I'm going to his barn to shoot the man's mule."

With that, Mantle drove like a madman to the barn, jumped out of the car, ran into the barn, and shot the old mule. But to his surprise, Mantle heard two more shots ring out behind him. Whirling around he saw Billy Martin with his rifle smoking. "What are you doing?" Mantle asked. Martin yelled back in anger, "I got two of his cows."

The Golden Rule

Little wonder Jesus said that anyone who is angry with his brother will be subject to judgment. Anger can kill, more than just a couple of cows. But anger is symptomatic of a deeper problem. People can't seem to get along with one another. When we do not treat each other charitably, we face the judgment that our choice brings.

"Do unto others as you would have them do unto you" is more than the Golden Rule; it is one of the secrets to getting our prayers answered. Jesus continued, "Therefore, if you are offering your gift at the altar and there remember that your brother has something against you, leave your gift there in front of the altar. First go and be reconciled to your brother; then come and offer your gift" (Matt. 5:23–24).

God absolutely refuses to accept sacrifices from us—even the sacrifice of our prayers—if we are at odds with others. John Wesley said, "That your prayer may have its full weight with God, see that ye be in charity with all men. For, otherwise, it is more likely to bring a curse than a blessing on your own head; nor can you expect to receive any blessing from God while you have not charity towards your neighbour."[11]

That's exactly what Jesus said to those at the altar. It's as if God were asserting, "Don't pray to me until you get right with each other!" Richard Sibbes was right when he said,

"God would rather have no sacrifice than no charity."[12] We should remember that.

Jesus in Neighbor's Clothes

It's little wonder that how we treat others impacts how God treats us when we pray. Think in whose name we pray and whom we offend when we don't get along with others. Jesus said, "I will do whatever you ask in my name" (John 14:13). "You may ask me for anything in my name, and I will do it" (John 14:14). "My Father will give you whatever you ask in my name" (John 16:23). Those are pretty astonishing promises. Each of them carries with it the one qualifier that we must ask in Jesus' name.

Jesus taught that "in my name" is the key to getting along with others as well. We live charitably when we treat others as we would treat Jesus. The Master said, "Anyone who gives you a cup of water in my name . . . will certainly not lose his reward" (Mark 9:41). Charity that arises out of love for Jesus will communicate love for others. Again Jesus said, "Whoever welcomes one of these little children in my name welcomes me" (Mark 9:37).

Accepting others can never really happen until we realize that failure to accept others is failure to accept Jesus. Jesus even said that when we gather together with other believers, we gather in his name. "For where two or three come together in my name, there am I with them" (Matt. 18:20). What's the clear implication? When we come together as a church and charity is absent, so is the Lord.

Living in charity with Jesus means living in charity with our friends and family. After all, Jesus lives next door to each of us. If we give a cup of water to a thirsty man, we give a cup of water to Jesus. If we treat a child with respect, we treat Jesus with respect. If we gather with others in a spirit of love, we gather with Jesus. All these others are Jesus in neighbor's clothes.

Hindered Relationships/Hindered Prayers

Doing good to our brothers and sisters means doing good to Jesus (Matt. 25:31–46). But it means much more. It means giving our prayers a better than even chance. As Bill Hybels says, "There's no point in trying to pray if we are engaged in ongoing conflict with a family member, a co-worker, a neighbor, a friend. 'Anyone who claims to be in the light but hates his brother is still in the darkness' (1 John 2:9). God will listen when you come out into the light, confess the sins that drove you and the other person apart and attempt to mend the relationship."[13]

God is committed to healing broken relationships, whether it is our own fractured relationship with him or our fractured relationships with others. He is Jehovah Rapha, the God who heals. His specialty is healing relationships that have been hammered flat on the anvil of anger. If God can heal the strained relationship between brothers Jacob and Esau (Gen. 31–32), between the prodigal son and his father (Luke 15:11–31), between Jews and Gentiles (Eph. 2:11–22), he can heal the fractured, strained relationships in our life.

When your relationships are hindered, your prayers are hindered as well. An important element in getting through to God is getting right with others. Leave your prayers on the altar. Go to that person with whom you have a bruised relationship and make it right. Confess your sinful attitudes toward him or her, ask for forgiveness, and start over. Then come back to your prayers. See if you don't have a whole new feeling of freedom and fortune.

The High Cost of Neglect

I have never considered myself poor. Perhaps you haven't either, for which we must thank the Lord. My father pastored two small churches when I was growing up, and together they didn't pay us enough to live on. We raised chickens to supplement our income. We had very little and worked very hard, but I wouldn't say we were poor.

My seminary friend, an African-American who grew up in urban poverty, said his family didn't know they were poor until the government told them they were. Our backgrounds were very different. I grew up in the country; he was raised in the city. I am white; he is black. I was from the East; he was from the South. Still, when we sat chatting over coffee one day discussing our childhoods and what it meant to be poor, neither of us thought we were poverty stricken.

But poverty is real—very real. With the softening of the job market, rapid change in technology, and subsequent upheaval in skilled labor needs, there has been a growing trend in America to add another layer on the poverty scale—the middle class poor. Sounds like an oxymoron, I know. But whether you have never had anything or you have had it and lost it, if you are experiencing the pain of poverty right now, you know how much you feel neglected.

Providing for the Poor

In some churches the social needs of society have replaced the pure message of the gospel, while in others the preaching of the gospel has so focused on the future that present needs have gone unnoticed. Many Christians forget the poor. If we do not encounter them on a daily basis, it's as if they do not exist. The pendulum needs to swing closer to the center.

The poor have always been on God's heart. Ancient Israel was told to leave the ground fallow the seventh year so the poor could glean from it (Exod. 23:10). They were not to harvest from their vineyards a second time but to leave some grapes for the poor (Lev. 19:10). God required the Jews to tend to the needs of the poor. "If there is a poor man among your brothers . . . do not be hardhearted or tightfisted toward your poor brother" (Deut. 15:7).

Ultimate relief for the poor comes from the Lord himself (see 1 Sam. 2:7–8; Ps. 72:12–13; Isa. 41:17), yet God commands us to help relieve poverty. "Rescue the weak and needy; deliver them from the hand of the wicked" (Ps. 82:4). "Do not oppress the widow or the fatherless, the alien or the poor" (Zech. 7:10). As if anticipating Jesus' statement to his disciples about the universal presence of the poor (John 12:2–8), Deuteronomy 15:11 advises, "There will always be poor people in the land. Therefore I command you to be openhanded toward your brothers and toward the poor and needy in your land."

What would be the fate of anyone who neglected to help the poor? In charging that the wicked "has oppressed the poor and left them destitute" (Job 20:19), Zophar implied that Job's calamities were the result of forsaking the poor. Job's defense was that he "rescued the poor who cried for help" (29:12), was "a father to the needy" (29:16), never "denied the desires of the poor" (31:16), and had "heard the cry of the needy" (34:28). Job was an incredibly wealthy man with an equally incredible record of charity to the poor. He knew helping the poor was his responsibility. But there's more.

The Christian Poor

In the New Testament, preaching the gospel and helping the poor were not antithetical activities. Helping the poor was an outgrowth of the gospel, not a substitute for it. No one is saved by climbing out of the hole of poverty or by helping others crawl out of that hole. When Jesus told the rich young ruler to "sell everything you have and give to the poor" (Mark 10:21), he was not describing the salvation road to heaven. He was counseling the young man to get rid of everything that gave a false confidence of salvation. Zacchaeus gave half his goods to the poor *because* he was a changed man, not *to become* a changed man (Luke 19:8). Paul knew that caring for the poor was ultimately an act of Christian love, and without that love, even giving to the poor was unfulfilling (1 Cor. 13:3).

Christians have a special responsibility to other Christians who are poor. When James, Peter, and John gave their blessing for Paul to preach to the Gentiles, they issued one caution to him. In his own words Paul remembers, "All they asked was that we should continue to remember the poor, the very thing I was eager to do" (Gal. 2:10). Paul proved his eagerness by collecting money from the Christians in Galatia and Greece for the poor and needy Christians in Jerusalem (1 Cor. 16:1–4). That's more than mere concern. Paul was living charitably toward the poor, touched with their need, grieved by their anguish, active in their relief.

The Poor and Our Prayers

The benefits that accrue from caring for the poor are not one-way benefits. The street of blessing runs both ways.

Much of the wisdom of the wealthy Solomon, expressed in the Book of Proverbs, concerns the blessing of relating to those who are poor: "Blessed is he who is kind to the needy" (14:21); "Whoever is kind to the needy honors God" (14:31); "He who is kind to the poor lends to the LORD" (19:17); "A generous man will himself be blessed, for he shares his food with the poor" (22:9). In fact, a faulty relationship with the poor can spell disaster for our own financial well-being. Solomon warns, "He who gives to the poor will lack nothing, but he who closes his eyes to them receives many curses" (Prov. 28:27).

We are ill-motivated if we help the poor so that we will be blessed, but we are equally ill-blessed if we are not motivated to help the poor. We help another family in our church because we love them. We do what Jesus would have done. But there is a return for us, and that return is more than blessing. It affects whether or not God answers our prayers.

Tucked away in what Solomon says about our relationship with the poor is this eye-opening verse: "If a man shuts his ears to the cry of the poor, he too will cry out and not be answered" (Prov. 21:13).

One of the faulty relationships that can prevent our prayers from being answered is a faulty relationship with those around us who are in need. Think about it. Is there someone in your neighborhood who is struggling? Someone who could use a little help in cutting her lawn because she is a single parent who cannot afford to get her broken lawn mower fixed? Do you have a lawn mower? Presto! An opportunity to have your prayers answered. Is there a family in your church who says they don't need charity but could use some friends acting charitably toward them? Voilà! An opportunity to have your prayers answered.

Don't allow a callous, uncaring attitude toward those less fortunate than you spoil your prayers. Get God's ear. One of the ways to do that is to open your heart and your checkbook to the poor. If your prayers aren't getting answered the way you want, check to see if you're doing all God wants. The poor need you, and you need answers to your prayers. Your response to one is the key to God's response to the other.

The High Cost of Family Feuds

Now, the pièce de résistance of faulty relationships and unanswered prayer. Believe it or not, the Bible says that how we get along with others in our family has a bearing on whether or not God answers our prayers. Faulty relationships between husbands and wives can be a detriment to answered prayer.

Cameron Thompson sets the scene somewhat descriptively when he says, "Many men who are angels in public and devils at home wonder why their prayers are not answered. Wives who are jealous and sarcastic and given to pouting and complaining marvel when their prayers freeze on the ceiling and drip back down their neck."[14] Picturesque or not, the point is clear. Family feuds are a wet blanket on the effectiveness of our prayer life.

Sex and Marriage

Sex was designed by God for our pleasure and therefore placed by him within the confines of the protective circle of marriage. God ordained marriage for the lasting benefit of humankind. But, as with everything else human beings have touched, both sex and marriage have been blemished by sin. Today sex outside of marriage is as common as sex within marriage, and often the result is the disintegration of marriage and, subsequently, the family. Unfaithfulness carries with it a very high price.

In order to prevent the breakup of marriage and preserve the sanctity of the home, God has given some rules and guidelines for husbands and wives to follow. If we follow these guidelines, there will be peace and harmony in our homes; if we abandon the rules, well, we have homes like we have today.

One set of God's guidelines is found in 1 Peter 3:1–7. This passage treats the relationship between a husband and wife. Getting along in the family brings great blessing, but getting along means getting along in God's way. Here is a paraphrase of God's way: "You wives, be submissive to your own husbands. Your real beauty is not what you wear on the outside but rather who you are on the inside. God sees your unfading beauty as a gentle and quiet spirit, and so will your husband. Likewise you husbands, be considerate of the needs of your wife. Treat her with the respect she deserves because together you are partners, joint-heirs of the gracious gift of eternal life."

And suddenly, there it is—a bombshell. After these guidelines there is another clause that, frankly, I missed the first hundred or so times I read this passage. Peter doesn't give God's guidelines just so we have harmony in the home; he gives them so that our prayers will be answered. Peter says we should live in marriage as God ordained, "so that nothing will hinder your prayers" (3:7).

That clause hit me like the "Pow," "Bam," "Zot" in a Batman comic book. How I treat my wife has a serious bearing on how God treats my prayers. If my relationship with her is faulty, my prayers are hindered.

Barricades and Barriers

Often the way we treat our spouse creates barricades and barriers in our marriage relationship. That's tragic. But rarely do we realize that a faulty family relationship also erects barricades and barriers on our prayer superhighway to God. Warren Wiersbe explains:

> The word "hindered" has an interesting meaning in the original. It means to break up a road so that the army can't get through. In ancient warfare, this method was often used. The soldiers would block the road with rocks, trees and other barriers to prevent the opposing army from advancing. Thus, 1 Peter 3:7 is telling husbands and wives that if they are not getting along with each other, their prayers will be hindered. They will be putting up barricades and barriers along the road that will prevent God from answering their prayers.[15]

Husbands and wives need to pray with each other. Family prayer, in which a husband takes his wife's hand and together they pray to God, is a singularly intimate act. It is far more than spiritual or sexual; it is divine. It's as if the three of you—husband, wife, and God—were holding hands and agreeing with each other in peace and harmony. I cannot pray when I am angry with my wife, and frankly, I don't want her to pray when she is angry with me. Our relationship must be strong or our prayers will not be.

So, be careful how you treat one another. A faulty relationship between husbands and wives does far more damage than adding disunity to the home. It sets up barricades on the highway to God. It deters answered prayer.

If you are not willing to live by God's guidelines, don't be surprised if he is unwilling to answer your prayers. Correcting a faulty relationship with others, with the poor, or with your spouse will keep your prayers from falling on deaf ears in heaven. Right your relationships and you make your prayers answerable.

What's a Person to Do?

How can you right a relationship? If you are suffering from this prayer blocker, what can you do about it? How can your relationships be repaired? The steps are much easier to distinguish than to do, but let's take a stab at both.

Recognize that it takes two to make a meaningful relationship. A relationship is like the tango—it takes two. One person can relate to another, but they do not have a relationship unless the other relates in return. Further, in any faulty relationship there is no totally innocent party. One may be more guilty than the other, but every sincere seeker of a repaired relationship can identify areas in which he or she has contributed to the flaws in that relationship.

Someone has to make the first move. Let that someone be you. Regardless of which relationship is faulty—husband/wife, mother/daughter, father/friend, have/have not—if you don't make the first move toward reconciliation, it's likely no move will be made. Jesus said, "If your brother [mother, daughter, husband, wife, neighbor, boss, etc.] sins against you, go and show him his fault, just between the two of you" (Matt. 18:15). The first move is always yours.

Be a bridge, not a barricade. Talk with the one whose relationship with you is in disrepair, but begin by opening doors, not shutting them. Never say, "You've done this and I am offended. I demand an apology." That's not a bridge; that's a barricade. Admit that you've been wrong too. Sincerely apologize and pave the way for a reciprocal apology. Don't go beyond the truth in accepting blame, but don't hide the truth either.

Invest in enrichment. For years my lawn looked pretty sick until I had a professional lawn service begin a regular treatment program. You ought to see my lawn now. The same is true with relationships. If yours is a little sick, put some vitamins into it. Give it some enrichment. If this relationship is important to you, spend some time with this person in prayer, in one-on-one enrichment in God's Word, in sharing joys and heartaches.

Faulty relationships are prayer blockers that are largely within your control. If you're not getting answers from God, take an honest look at your relationships with your family, church, and neighbors. If they are in disrepair, formulate a plan for reconstruction. Work your plan. Your prayers depend on it.

Prayer

Blocker #**5**

God doesn't answer when

We Need a Faith Lift

> Faith is deliberate confidence in the character of God whose ways you may not understand at the time.
>
> Oswald Chambers

Everyone knows how important faith is. Just ask them. We put our faith in the skill of airline pilots, the safety of bridges spanning mighty rivers, and the cleanliness of kitchens in restaurants. We may never have flown that airline, crossed that river, or eaten at that restaurant before, yet we have faith in people and things we've never met or encountered.

Faith is a part of life. If we're going to live with any degree of normalcy, we have to have faith in people and things. That's true for the Bible as well. Faith is a dominant theme in the Bible. The Hebrew noun or adjective for *faith* is used in the Old Testament more than fifty times, but it's not until the New Testament that faith comes into full bloom. The Greek noun or adjective is used more than three hundred times.

As common as faith is, it's difficult to define. Webster says faith is a "firm belief in something for which there is no proof."[16] Someone even defined faith as "the power of believing what we know to be untrue," to which C. S. Lewis countered that faith is "the power of continuing to believe what we once honestly thought to be true until cogent reasons for honestly changing our minds are brought before us."[17]

Most definitions of faith relate little to God. For example, there is a popular definition that says faith is the daring of the soul to go farther than it can see. But what has that to do with God? Faith that does not relate to God is not biblical faith. It is certainly not the kind of faith necessary if God is to answer our prayers.

I define faith as confidence in the righteous character of God that fosters trust and hope even when our circumstances foster doubt and despair. Isn't that what prayer is about? Our circumstances look grim, so we pray to God in faith, trusting his righteous character to do what is best for us.

In this chapter we want to focus on a lack of faith as a significant prayer blocker. Does failure to believe God have anything to do with our prayers not being answered? One of the classic biblical passages on faith speaks directly to this issue:

> If any of you lacks wisdom, he should ask God, who gives generously to all without finding fault, and it will be given to him. But when he asks, he must believe and not doubt, because he who doubts is like a wave of the sea, blown and tossed by the wind. That man should not think he will receive anything from the Lord; he is a double-minded man, unstable in all he does.
>
> James 1:5–7

The words of James are punctuated with implications of faith. If we have a need, we must ask God for help. God will give us what we need if we believe him. If we don't believe him, we are torturously tossed about by our own doubt.

Here is James's bottom line about prayer and faith: Pray, believe, and run to first base with God's blessing; pray, doubt, and strike three, you're out. It's that simple.

If faith in God makes the difference between answered and unanswered prayer, we dare not pray without first investigating our own faith. We need to see if some flaw of faith keeps God from answering our prayers.

What Kind of Faith?

It can be confusing when we read about faith in the Bible. The writers speak of the word of faith (Rom. 10:8), the measure of faith (Rom. 12:3), the spirit of faith (2 Cor. 4:13), the assurance of faith (Heb. 10:22), and so much more. It seems that everything in our Christian life relates to faith, and that includes prayer.

The Gift of Faith

Paul wrote to the Corinthian church about spiritual gifts. One of those is the gift of faith (1 Cor. 12:9). Like the other gifts, the Holy Spirit graciously gives the gift of faith to whomever he chooses (1 Cor. 12:11). Not everyone receives this gift.

If faith is your gift, how would you know? No theological answers here, just the facts. You would believe God when no one else was able. Your faith in God would be stronger than you could ordinarily explain. This is not just "hope against hope" faith, but faith gifted to you by God.

John had not been feeling well for months. To his wife, Evelyn, and their children, John Jr. and Terri, it was evident that something was seriously wrong. When John finally went to the doctor, his worst fears were confirmed. He had a rapidly growing cancer.

John began radiation treatments. At the same time, his family and he prayed for healing. Terri was especially intense in her prayers. She spent an hour or more each day reading her Bible, claiming the promises of God, and praying for her dad. Soon Terri became convinced that God was going to heal him.

The others had confidence that God could heal John too, but Terri had something more than confidence. She had God's gift of faith. She had never been more certain of anything in her life. And she was right. John's cancer disappeared and never returned.

But you say, "It's hard for me to believe God. I don't have the gift of faith." Certainly it would be nice to have the gift of faith, but not everyone does.

The Holy Spirit may not choose to give you this special gift. It doesn't matter. That's not what the writer of Hebrews had in mind when he said, "Without faith it is impossible to please God" (Heb. 11:6). If it were, only those with this particular gift would be pleasing to God, and that's just not true. You don't need the gift of faith to believe God, but you do need faith.

The Grace of Faith

We are saved by grace (Eph. 2:8); we serve in grace (Heb. 12:28 KJV); we sing with grace (Col. 3:16 KJV). Often the word *grace* is used of the virtues that guide our Christian life. Paul referred to the grace of giving (2 Cor. 8:7). He urged, "Let your conversation be always full of grace, seasoned with salt" (Col. 4:6). Because grace relates to those virtues by which we please God, it's little wonder Peter prayed, "But grow in the grace and knowledge of our Lord and Savior Jesus Christ" (2 Peter 3:18).

We do not need a special gift of faith to have our prayers answered. God gives that gift only to a few. But we do need the grace of faith, and that's available to every believer. This simply means we have adopted a lifestyle of faith, trusting the promises of God in every area of our life.

Christians need to live the way we were saved—by faith. It's in this daily faith that we need a faith lift, and it's by God's grace that we receive this lift. God has made significant promises to us, but we need our faith lifted to claim them in prayer. Without such a lift, prayer is blocked.

Weak Faith

Of God's promises and faith Harold Lindsell says, "When we pray for peace of heart and mind and do not have faith to believe this petition will be answered, it is sin for there is a promise to that effect (Phil. 4:5–7). If we pray for the necessities of life without faith to believe that God will supply them, this is sin for there is a promise to that effect (Matt. 6:33)."[18]

Lindsell is right. The prayer that rises out of faith hitches its star to God's promises. We don't need a special gift to trust God's promises. Jesus said, "If you have faith as small as a mustard seed, you can say to this mountain, 'Move from here to there' and it will move. Nothing will be impossible for you" (Matt. 17:20–21).

The failure of faith is a major contributor to the failure of prayer. It is a debilitating prayer blocker. But it doesn't have to be. Our faith may not be gigantic, but as a Christian, faith is already present in our life by God's grace. What we need is a faith lift, and the best way to get that is to focus on God and his promises.

Misplaced Faith

Some people need a faith lift because they've been putting their faith in the wrong place. They've been relying on the means, not the end. They've gotten tangled up in the process, not the promises. They've been putting their coins in the wrong machine.

You're thirsty. You need a soft drink. Luckily, there's a pop machine nearby. You have change in your pocket. You're all set. But instead of putting your change in the pop machine, you mistakenly drop it in the candy machine. You're disappointed. No soft drinks in the candy machine. You hit the coin return but, as usual, it's jammed. You can have change in your pocket and still not meet your needs if you don't put that change in the right place.

That's the way it is with faith. We can have faith and still not have our needs met if we put our faith in the wrong place.

Some people have faith in faith. Perhaps they've been watching too much television. They've heard preachers and healers talk about the power of faith. They know faith is the key, so they've been led to believe that if they just have enough faith, God will do anything. But that's not what the Bible says.

Often faith healers ask people at their crusades if they have faith. The answer is always yes. Sometimes these folks are genuinely healed; other times they are not. If no healing takes place, the healer sometimes chides, "Obviously you didn't have enough faith or you would have been healed." But that's having faith in faith. No one was ever healed by having too much or too little faith in faith. Just having faith is not enough. Our faith must be directed toward the right end. That right end is God.

Others believe that prayer is their fiber-optic link with God, and they have faith in it. They believe in prayer. They have faith that their prayers will be answered.

But prayer is the system; God is the source. Sometimes the system fails those who use it. When it does, these people are tempted to try a new system, like channeling or mediums. But prayer is the only phone line in town that gets through to God.

If we make prayer the object of our faith, we will come up short every time. It's like trusting an airplane to get us to our destination instead of trusting the pilot. The airplane is just the vehicle; it's the pilot who gets us safely to our destination.

Nowhere in Scripture are we exhorted to put our faith in prayer, in faith, or in anything but God. Prayer is not the answer; God is the answer. Faith is but a grace in our lives; God is the guarantee of that grace. In spite of the motto, prayer does not change things; God changes things. The only appropriate place for your faith is in God.

Have Faith in God

Jesus taught, "Have faith in God" (Mark 11:22). Obviously there is no reason to pray if we don't believe God can hear us, and there is no reason to believe he will hear us if we don't believe he is real. That drives us to a more basic question: How can God answer our prayers if there is no God? Jesus' words, "Have faith in God," require some reflection on the character of God.

If you want your prayers to be answered, have faith in the God who is there, able, and willing.

The God Who Is There

Hebrews 11:6 says, "And without faith it is impossible to please God." But the verse doesn't stop there. "Because anyone who comes to him must believe that he exists and that he rewards those who earnestly seek him."

If you do not believe God exists, how can you have faith in him? The kind of faith that is the basis for answered prayer is not a spiritual cousin to wishful thinking. God is not inclined to answer prayers that begin, "God, if you're out there, listen to me." That's not faith in God; that's a shot in the dark.

If you have doubts about God's existence, go to his Word before you pray. Absorb the testimony of your Bible about God. Allow the Holy Spirit to speak to you about the God who is there. Answered prayer begins with the confidence that God is alive and he hears you when you pray.

The God Who Is Able

To believe that God exists is one thing, to believe that he is able to answer your prayers is quite another. Is God big enough to tackle the magnitude of your need? How big is God? How able is he to answer your prayers?

One day Jesus encountered two blind men who desperately wanted to be healed. They cried out, "Have mercy on us, Son of David!" Jesus asked, "Do you believe that I am able to do this?" When they responded affirmatively, he touched their eyes and said, "According to your faith will it be done to you" (Matt. 9:27–29). They were healed because they believed Jesus was able to heal them. If you're not sure God is able to answer your prayers, but you've decided it can't hurt to pray anyway, don't expect God to answer you. Answered prayer arises from faith that God is able to answer.

Hannah wanted a child more than anything, but she was barren. With her face stained with tears, she went to the house of God to pour out her heart: "O LORD Almighty, if you will only look upon your servant's misery and remember me, and not forget your servant but give her a son, then I will give him to the LORD for all the days of his life" (1 Sam. 1:11). Hannah was convinced God was able to answer her prayer. A year later, the birth of her son, Samuel, was living proof that it pays to have faith that God is able.

Not being sure God is able to answer you is a real prayer blocker. Having faith in God means you believe he is there, he hears your prayers, and he has the power to answer them.

The God Who Is Willing

Have you ever prayed but God didn't answer? Of course you have. We all have. That's what this book is about. Was it because you did not believe in God? Likely not. Was it because you did not think he was able to answer your prayers? Maybe not. So why didn't he answer? God is there,

God is able, and yet he may still not be willing to answer your prayers.

We have a sense of "oughtness" about God—he is a good God; he ought to answer this prayer. But sifting God through an "oughtness" grid discredits his sovereignty.

Jesus had been teaching large crowds on the hills rising from the Sea of Galilee. His Sermon on the Mount is recorded in Matthew 5–7. When he finished his discourse, the Savior came down from the mountain, and there before him fell a man eaten away by leprosy. He begged, "Lord, if you are willing, you can make me clean" (Matt. 8:2).

This leper was convinced Jesus could heal him. Ability was not the issue; the issue was will. Was Jesus willing to heal him? The leper had come to grips with something about faith that many of us have not yet grasped. The God who is there, the God who is able, is not always willing to answer our prayers. He has his own reasons for answering prayer, and his reasons are not always your reasons (Isa. 55:8–9). But you must accept that, on occasion, God refuses to answer, and he doesn't tell you why. Your request simply was not his will.

Before You Pray

Prayer is an act of faith. The apostle John says, "This is the confidence we have in approaching God: that if we ask anything according to his will, he hears us. And if we know that he hears us—whatever we ask—we know that we have what we asked of him" (1 John 5:14–15). That's not just faith; it's confident faith. As Lehman Strauss observed, "There is no point at all in coming to God in prayer if we do not have confidence in Him."[19]

George Mueller was a man of great faith and a man of prayer. He and the staff at his orphanage in Bristol, England, had a lifelong record of believing God and seeing answers to their prayers—more than twenty-five thousand times. When asked by a friend to explain his secret, Mueller said, "Have faith in God." That should be your secret too. If you want answers to your prayers, have faith in God. Asking something of God is an act of faith—faith that God is there to hear you, that he is able to assist you, and that he is willing to answer you.

If you're in the market for a new car, do you walk on a lot and buy the first car you see? Of course not. You ask around to find out if the dealer is reputable. If you have some money to invest, do you just choose a broker from the yellow pages? That would be foolish. Again, you try to learn everything you can about your broker. If you want to pray in faith, do you just jump into prayer? Frequently we do. But first we should get to know the one we're praying to.

The great reformer, Martin Luther, suggested that our prayers should exercise "faith and confidence toward God" so that "we do not doubt that we shall be heard."[20] That's a pretty tall order for most of us. How can we have that kind of confidence in God? We need "pre-prayer faith." This is faith in the character of God before we pray so that when we pray we can pray in confidence. The Lord Jesus said, "Everything is possible for him who believes" (Mark 9:23).

Can you believe God for everything? Is your faith that strong? Maybe not. It wasn't always strong for Jesus' disciples either. Once they said to the Master, "Increase our faith!" (Luke 17:5). Even Jesus' closest followers sometimes needed a faith lift. If you're tired of too little faith being a prayer blocker, if you need a faith builder, what can be done before you pray to help build your faith? Here are some possibilities:

1. *Clear away the clutter in your life.* Sin is clutter, so before you pray, take out the trash. A purified life is the perfect place in which faith can grow. It's like a petri dish in which you control all the nutrients necessary for an organism to flourish. The less unwelcome bacteria found in the dish, the better chance the organism has to grow. By confessing your sin and

asking God to forgive you for that sin, you clear away the bacteria of your life, and your faith in God will grow strong.

2. *Spend an extended time reading your Bible before you pray.* Think about what you're reading. You don't have to understand everything; God promises a blessing to those who read his Word (Rev. 1:3). That blessing could be having your prayers answered. Reading the Bible with the honest intention of hearing from God and obeying what he says builds your faith. "Faith comes from hearing the message, and the message is heard through the word of Christ" (Rom. 10:17). Read and "hear" God's message for your life, and it will build your faith in God.

3. *Concentrate on the evidence that God is already working in your life.* If you are a Christian, think of how your life changed when God brought you from darkness to light. Build your faith. If you have moved from spiritual infancy along the road to spiritual maturity, chart how far you have come. Build your faith. If God has answered your prayers before, remember the joy his answers brought and build your faith. Concentrate on how God has already blessed you. Most of us would have stronger faith if we had stronger memories.

4. *Read the stories of others whose prayers have been answered.* Many biographies of great Christians are real faith builders. Read what God has done for others in answer to prayer and build your confidence that he will do the same for you. Start by reading Hebrews 11. Then read the biographical portions of the Bible that tell the stories of Abraham, Moses, Caleb, David, Jabez, Daniel, Peter, and Paul. Finally, snuggle into the biographies of George Mueller, Praying (John) Hyde, C. T. Studd, David Livingstone, Chuck Colson, and others. God is at work in the lives of his people. He wants to work in your life too.

5. *Become more intimate in your relationship with God.* One reason your faith may need a lift is that you don't know God very well. It's like talking to a stranger. People rarely open up to people they don't know. But a relationship with God

that reveals itself in a daily walk builds your faith in him. Jesus said, "If you remain in me and my words remain in you, ask whatever you wish, and it will be given you" (John 15:7). That's quite a promise, but it comes with a precondition. Intimate time with God before you pray encourages you that he will answer when you pray. Meet the condition and your faith in God will soar.

Getting answers requires faith in God before you begin to pray. While you are praying is not the time to begin sizing up God's ability to answer. Have faith in God before you pray.

Praying Prayers of Faith

You want God to answer your prayers and you've already taken some steps to build your faith. Now it's time to pray. What is it about prayer that demands faith? What can you do while praying to bolster your faith? Here are four secrets I've learned about how to pray prayers of faith.

Begin with Reverence

Our God is an awesome God. "How awesome is the LORD Most High, the great King over all the earth!" (Ps. 47:2). He is a majestic God. "O LORD, our Lord, how majestic is your name in all the earth!" (Ps. 8:1). When you pray to him, you ought to acknowledge his unmatchable character. That's why Jesus taught his disciples to begin their prayers, "Our Father in heaven, hallowed be your name" (Matt. 6:9).

Praying with faith means praying with confidence in the righteous character of God. Bow before him, worship and adore him. The great prayers of the Bible generally begin with this kind of adoration. Make it a part of your prayers and watch your faith build.

Pray the Promises

Another way to build your faith while praying is to pray the promises of God. Demonstrate to God that you take his Word seriously by quoting his promises to him while you pray. Read the promises from God in his Word. Pray the promises to God in response.

Here are some exceeding great and precious promises that I frequently pray to God: "Come near to God and he will come near to you" (James 4:8). "My God will meet all your needs according to his glorious riches in Christ Jesus" (Phil. 4:19). "When I am afraid, I will trust in you. In God, whose word I praise, in God I trust; I will not be afraid" (Ps. 56:3–4). "This is the confidence we have in approaching God: that if we ask anything according to his will, he hears us" (1 John 5:14). Pray God's promises when you pray. It's a great way to give your faith a lift.

Expand Your Faith

In his prophecy about God's future plans for Jerusalem, Isaiah borrowed a figure from the nomadic life of the bedouin: "Enlarge the place of your tent, stretch your tent curtains wide, do not hold back; lengthen your cords, strengthen your stakes" (Isa. 54:2). Like a nomad blessed of God with so many children that he had to enlarge his tent, God will one day bless Jerusalem in a way that will astound the world.

We too need to be enlarging our capacity to receive his blessing by enlarging our faith. Perhaps that's what the disciples meant when they prayed, "Increase our faith" (Luke 17:5). It's certainly what Jabez meant when he prayed, "Oh, that you would bless me and enlarge my territory!" (1 Chron. 4:10).

While you're praying is a good time to enlarge your tent. Try it. The next time you pray, allow God to expand your faith by lengthening the cords of your prayer requests and driving down the stakes of trust and confidence. After all, if he is "able to do immeasurably more than all we ask or imagine" (Eph. 3:20), isn't it time you went to God with a bigger tent?

End with Anticipation

Someone mused, "Blessed is he who expecteth nothing, for he shall not be disappointed." When you pray, is your final "Amen" just a "hello" to doubt? Do you sign off with the sigh, "Well, that probably didn't get me anywhere"? Or do you end your prayers in anticipation of an answer?

I have always believed that anticipation is half the fun of travel. When I go abroad, I get out a map, chart where I'm going, plan my itinerary, and spend weeks anticipating my journey. Anticipation is important in your prayer journey as well. Map out your requests, chart the course you think God may take you, and anticipate the results.

Once you have prayed, however, don't try to revise your itinerary; simply anticipate your destination. Remember, James says when you pray you must not doubt. If you do, you are like the wave of the sea, blown and tossed by the wind (James 1:6). That's like saying you are a traveler without a destination.

You should always demonstrate faith as you pray (see Matt. 21:22; Mark 11:24; John 14:14), but ending prayer with a ring of anticipation is a real faith builder. William W. Walford's hymn, "Sweet Hour of Prayer," includes these words of anticipation: "And since He bids me seek His face, Believe His Word and trust His grace, I'll cast on Him my ev'ry care, And wait for thee, sweet hour of prayer." End your prayers with the certain anticipation of God's response and you will build your faith.

What's a Person to Do?

Some people who have faith in God before they pray lose that faith if he doesn't answer quickly. If you pray in faith but allow your confidence to turn to doubt before God responds to your need, you become a prime candidate for unanswered prayer. Post-prayer faith is just as important as pre-prayer faith.

If you want God to answer your prayers, after you have prayed, pay close attention to these details:

Stay adjusted to the presence of the Holy Spirit. It is the Spirit of God who prays for us with inaudible, inexpressible sighs (Rom. 8:26–27). After you have long finished praying, he continues on your behalf. But you must remain adjusted to his presence within you. You do this by confessing your sin, repenting of it, and removing the grief your sin causes him (Eph. 4:30). Then you must be careful not to stifle the Spirit's work in your life (1 Thess. 5:19) by being uncooperative with him or unresponsive to his presence. Finally, you must allow the Holy Spirit to fill you with his power and presence daily (Eph. 5:18), to make you a clean vessel, and to enable you to be used by him.

Get busy for God. Hudson Taylor, renowned missionary to China, remarked, "Faith is reliance on the trustworthiness of those with whom we transact business. Our faith is the recognition of God's faithfulness. It is so blessed to leave our faith out of account, and to be so occupied with God's faithfulness that we cannot raise any question whatsoever."[21] Be occupied with God's faithfulness. Be busy in ways that God can demonstrate his response to your faith. Give him the opportunity to prove his faithfulness in your witness to your neighbor, in your preparation to teach your Bible study group, in your financial support of his work. When you remain active for God and focus on his faithfulness, you live the post-prayer life of faith.

Remember God's promises. Harken back to some of the great prayer promises of the Bible. Our memories help our faith to stay strong. Some of these promises are truly amazing. Take Mark 11:24 for example. Jesus said, "Whatever you ask for in prayer, believe that you have received it, and it will be yours." Our natural inclination is to tone down such statements because, of course, our prayers are subject to God's will and preconditions. Still, this is an amazingly inclusive promise. If after you pray you continue to remember God's promises, you will have ongoing faith that he will answer your prayer.

Don't require faithless confirmation. So often when people pray they tack on to their prayers, "And Lord, just give me a sign that you have heard me." By definition, requiring a sign is not praying in faith. Gideon wanted God to do some atmospheric tricks to confirm his will (Judg. 6:36–40), and God graciously was patient with the feebleness of Gideon's faith. However, Jesus constantly deprecated the seeking of a sign. When Thomas refused to believe Jesus had risen from the dead until he had the confirmation of his own senses, Jesus gently rebuked him (John 20:29). Either you have faith in God or you do not; don't badger him for external signs to supplement your faith.

Learn to rest in the character of God. "Trust in the LORD and do good. . . . Delight yourself in the LORD and he will give you the desires of your heart. Commit your way to the LORD; trust in him and he will do this. . . . Be still before the LORD and wait patiently for him" (Ps. 37:3–5, 7). There it is—the key for post-prayer faith. The Christian who does not doubt relaxes in the belief that God has heard him and will, in his own time, answer his prayer.

If the prayer offered in faith can make the sick person well (James 5:15), and the prayer offered in doubt can destabilize the Christian life (James 1:6–8), it appears that the choice of how you pray is left to you. Don't waver; rest. Don't question; trust. Don't worry; pray.

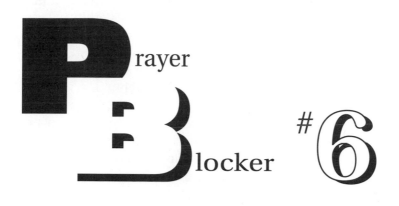

Prayer Blocker #6

God doesn't answer when

We Harbor an Unforgiving Spirit

It is in pardoning that we are pardoned.

St. Francis of Assisi

Prayer blockers come in all shapes and sizes. Some stand alone; some act in concert with others. Some work on certain people, some on others. But there is one prayer blocker that seems to possess universal potency. It has been called "the chief blockage to prayer."[22] It's an unforgiving spirit.

Robert Louis Stevenson tells a tragic tale of the failure to forgive in "Edinburgh: Picturesque Notes."[23] He writes of two spinster sisters who had a falling out over "some point of controversial divinity." They shared a single room, but their disagreement was so bitter they vowed never to speak a word to each other again. The two lived the rest of their miserable lives in spiteful silence. The sisters drew a chalk line down the middle of the room. "It bisected the doorway and the fireplace, so that each could go out and in, and do her cooking, without violating the territory of the other," said Stevenson. Their hatred divided the room into two equal but unfriendly halves. The world is filled with such malignant lines, as the people of Korea, Vietnam, and more recently, Bosnia can attest.

These Scottish sisters coexisted in their own unforgiving worlds. Each prepared her own meals, had her own visitors, and cleaned her own half of the room. At night they lay only inches apart, literally sleeping with the enemy. Stevenson says they engaged in their "hideous twin devotions, thumbing a pair of great Bibles, or praying aloud for each other's penitence." Forgiveness was never a consideration, and thus they never reconciled.

Forgive Us . . . As We Also Have Forgiven

The greatest prayer of the Bible, the Lord's Prayer, is a model for prayer, a guide to be followed by all who want to pray biblically and effectively. Matthew records it from the lips of Jesus in Matthew 6:9–13.

Not only does this prayer teach us how to address God, it also gives us categories of things to pray about:

Worship and adoration—"hallowed be your name"
Moral and ethical issues—"your will be done on earth"
Physical needs—"give us today our daily bread"
Spiritual needs—"deliver us from the evil one"
Relational needs—"forgive us our debts, as we also have forgiven our debtors"

Some of these petitions are easy. Who wouldn't want to revere the name of God or take our need for food to him? Others are not so easy. Asking not to be led into temptation is a pretty weighty petition. But one request stands above the rest in terms of difficulty; it's the Lord's Prayer's most difficult petition. "Forgive us our debts, as we also have for-given our debtors." That's hard praying.

St. Augustine called this request "the terrible petition," and with good reason. The interpretive possibilities for this petition are limited. It's like being faced with two options: You can be audited by the IRS and pay back taxes and heavy penalties, or you can go to jail. Neither option is attractive if you are a tax cheater.

Difficult Options

"The terrible petition" seems to imply that there is a di-rect relationship between our willingness to forgive others and our own forgiveness. I call this the *forgiven/forgive* rela-tionship. How are we to understand this petition? What was Jesus getting at when he commanded us to pray, "Forgive us our debts, as we also have forgiven our debtors"?

Two interpretive possibilities immediately come to mind. Jesus could have meant, "Forgive us our debts to the same ex-tent we have forgiven others." This is forgiveness by degree. To the degree that we forgive others, we petition God to forgive us.

My initial response to this possibility is not positive. I'm not sure I want to make this request. We all like to pick and choose whom and what we will forgive. For example, for-giveness flows freely for a husband's extravagance in pur-chasing too many Christmas gifts but slows dramatically for an office indiscretion. If repentance is real and confession is genuine, we cannot simply choose to forgive some sins and not others. That's forgiveness by degree. Pick-and-choose forgiveness is not something we want from God. None of us wants him to forgive some of our sins and not others. Yet this is how we respond to others. If we want God's forgiveness to the fullest extent, we must forgive to the fullest extent.

We also do not want God to adopt what we might call "per-centage forgiveness." A husband's anger boils over when his wife maxes out their credit cards. After that she only enjoys 80 percent forgiveness from him. But what good is that? None of us wants anything but 100 percent forgiveness. Since we want nothing less than 100 percent forgiveness from God, we are not keen to pray, "Forgive us our debts, to the same extent we have forgiven others."

The other interpretive possibility is that Jesus could have meant, "Forgive us our debts in the same way we have forgiven others." This is forgiveness by pattern. It's saying to God, "I'm asking you to forgive me in the same way I have forgiven others. If I have grudgingly forgiven others, grudgingly forgive me. If I have conditionally forgiven others, conditionally forgive me." Again, who of us wants to pray, "Forgive us our debts in the same way we have forgiven others"?

If we have not completely and honestly forgiven others, it is a death wish to pray that God will forgive us the same way. R. Kent Hughes agrees. "The Lord's Prayer can actually become to us a self-inflicted curse—a prayer of doom instead of blessing! What we are really praying may actually sound something like this: 'I beseech you, Lord, deal with me as I deal with my neighbor. He has been ungrateful to me, yet I cannot overlook his ingratitude. Deal with me, Lord, as I do him.'"[24] Failure to forgive is devastating to getting answers to prayer.

The Great Prayer Appendix

Sometimes when writing a book an author treats a subject that needs additional affirmation or elucidation. If he or she has only a small amount to add, the author can always add an endnote at the end of the chapter. But if he or she has much more to say or wants to accent what was said, the author can opt for an appendix at the end of the book. It appears as if that's what Jesus did after teaching his disciples the Lord's Prayer. He added an appendix on forgiveness.

The appendix may appear to be brief, but given Jesus' original words about forgiveness in the prayer (thirteen words in Greek), this appendix is really quite exhaustive (thirty-three words in Greek). "For if you forgive men when they sin against you, your heavenly Father will also forgive you. But if you do not forgive men their sins, your Father will not forgive your sins" (Matt. 6:14–15).

From this appendix we might draw the conclusion that forgiving others precedes God's forgiving us. That isn't true, of course, because without God's gracious forgiveness we would never truly be able to forgive others. The original petition in the Lord's Prayer—"Forgive us our debts, as we also have forgiven our debtors"—is first and foremost a prayer for forgiveness, our forgiveness. It is an admission that our great need is forgiveness from God for our sins. Our subsequent responsibility is to forgive others in the same way and to the same extent that we have been forgiven.

Does this appendix imply that if we fail to forgive after God has forgiven us he will rescind his gracious forgiveness for our sins? Not in the least. Our salvation is never conditional on what we do after we are saved but on what Jesus Christ did at Calvary before we were saved. Still, once we have been saved, there is a haunting responsibility to forgive as we have been forgiven. Forgiveness is the fruit of salvation, not the ground for it.

William Hendriksen observes, "Though in the teaching not only of Paul (Rom. 3:24; Eph. 2:8; Titus 3:5) but certainly also of Christ (Matt. 5:1–6; 18:27; Luke 18:13) salvation rests not on human accomplishments but solely on the grace and mercy of God, this does not mean that there is nothing to do for those who receive it. They must believe. Included in this faith is the eagerness to forgive. Unless the listeners forgive men their trespasses, they themselves will remain unpardoned."[25]

The faith that truly believes in the need for a Savior comes from a heart broken by sin and ready to forgive as it has been forgiven. When we are mindful that salvation faith is not "fire-escape" faith but repentant faith, we begin to understand that there is no real proof of our being forgiven unless we are willing to forgive. That's what Jesus was teaching.

The Prayer Link

What does all this have to do with God answering our prayers? Just this. Look at the context. The initial reference to forgiven/forgive is in the Lord's Prayer. In fact, it is right in the middle of the three petitions of that prayer that relate to us. It is central to our daily needs. It is also central to answered prayer.

Given the context of Jesus' forgiven/forgive teaching and that he immediately followed his pattern prayer with an appendix on that subject, we are left with the inescapable conclusion that failure to forgive is a strong deterrent to God hearing and answering our prayers. An unforgiving spirit deadens the soul, hardens the heart, and denies our access to God.

When we are unforgiving and cannot honestly pray the Lord's Prayer's "terrible petition," we have slammed shut the door to answered prayer. Only a willingness to forgive as we have been forgiven can open that door again, and God is anxious to have the door opened.

What Is Forgiveness?

Perhaps we should have begun this chapter by defining *forgiveness.* Confused minds and conflicting views about the nature of forgiveness only add crackling interference on our fiber-optic line to heaven. If we don't know what forgiveness is, how will we know if we have forgiven someone and made our prayers answerable?

I have read dozens of books on forgiveness. Most of them were filled with good advice. They were biblical in nature and warm in heart. But after reading them I asked, "What is forgiveness?" and time and again was left flat. Not that definitions were lacking, but they didn't have the ring of clarity and inclusiveness that I was looking for.

Then I discovered Wendell E. Miller's book *Forgiveness: The Power and the Puzzles.*[26] Miller is cofounder of the Biblical Counseling Association of Warsaw, Indiana. In his book, Miller unravels the Scriptures relating to forgiveness, some of which appear to contradict each other (but in fact do not). He introduces new vocabulary to shine light on old truths from what the Bible says about forgiven/forgive. Most of the following discussion about the character of forgiveness I owe to his good thinking.

Coming to Terms

Let's start at the beginning. What is forgiveness? What did it mean in New Testament times? What words did Bible writers use to describe forgiveness? The basic meaning of New Testament words for *forgiveness* is "to release."

Several forms of the Greek verb *aphiemi* are used for God's forgiveness of man (e.g., Matt. 6:12–15; Mark 11:25; Luke 5:21; 1 John 1:9). The word is also used of man's forgiveness of man. Some forms of the verb *charizomai* are also used of God's forgiveness and man's forgiveness (e.g., Luke 7:43; 2 Cor. 2:10; Eph. 4:32; Col. 3:13). From these verbs we learn that when we forgive someone, we release him or her from the hurt he or she has done to us and from any consequences of that hurt.

Forgiveness is like throwing a dove into the air. With that upward swing of our arms and the opening of our hands, a bird that once was in our grasp is suddenly given wing to freedom. That's what forgiveness is. It's releasing to freedom something that we have held tightly since it came to us.

God Had Plenty to Forgive

The very thought that God forgives implies a need to forgive. We created that need when our first parents sinned in the Garden of Eden and joined Satan's rebellion against God. That original sin affected all of us. Their disobedience was our disobedience (Rom. 5:12–21). Fellowship with God was broken. Once he had walked and talked with Adam in the cool of the day (Gen. 3:8), but after they disobeyed God, Adam and Eve were expelled from the Garden and banned from immediate access to God (Gen. 3:24).

There was plenty to forgive, but how could God forgive? Would he just forget about our sin? That wouldn't work. Simply forgetting about sin could never restore broken fellowship. There had to be another way, and there was. God required a perfect blood sacrifice as payment for our sin. Immediately there was a problem. How could you or I provide a *perfect* sacrifice? Only God is perfect.

That's it! God would both require the blood of a perfect sacrifice to appease his anger (Lev. 17:11) and ask his Son, Jesus Christ, to be that sacrifice. At a place called Calvary, "God made him who had no sin to be sin for us, so that in him we might become the righteousness of God" (2 Cor. 5:21). God didn't sweep our sin under the cosmic carpet; he came to earth to die in our place. He made the payment for our sin himself. How very unlike our thinking; how very much like his (see Isa. 55:8–9).

Mission Accomplished

When Jesus Christ gave his life for our sins, he accomplished many things, four of which are important to our investigation into the relationship between forgiveness and answered prayer.

1. *Christ secured initial judicial forgiveness from God.* That means his shed blood secured our release from the penalty of sin (Rom. 6:23). It is now possible for us to be justified, declared by God and treated as if we were righteous (Rom.

4:3–5). That's judicial forgiveness—a legal release from the penalty of sin.

But such forgiveness is conditional. Jesus provided for forgiveness by his death, but it is only when we trust what he did at Calvary and ask him to be our Savior that forgiveness is ours.

2. *Jesus' death restored our broken fellowship with God.* Miller calls this "initial fellowship forgiveness." What was lost in Eden was regained at Calvary. We were reconciled to God (Col. 1:21–22). Our estranged relationship was changed by Jesus' loving, sacrificial act on the cross. We have access to God once more.

But this type of fellowship is also conditional. Again, the condition is that we must trust Jesus Christ as Savior. When we receive the benefits of Christ's atonement, we also receive the benefits of restored fellowship with God.

3. *The death of Christ secured repetitive judicial forgiveness for us.*[27] This means that his death not only secured forgiveness for the sins we committed before salvation, it also secured forgiveness for every sin we've committed since becoming a Christian. The blood of Christ is fully capable of atoning for the sin we find in our lives today. What his atonement did at Calvary, it continues to do today.

Unlike our initial forgiveness at salvation, this continuing forgiveness is unconditional. We do not have to ask Jesus to be our Savior again each time we sin, nor does he have to return to the cross to make payment for each sin. This requires Jesus' work as Advocate, not as Savior. "But if anybody does sin, we have one who speaks to the Father in our defense—Jesus Christ, the Righteous One" (1 John 2:1). There is no condition here. It is part of the daily benefit of what Jesus accomplished on the cross.

4. *Jesus' sacrifice at Calvary secured repetitive fellowship forgiveness.*[28] This means that after we are saved, sin sometimes strains our fellowship with God. The blood of Jesus Christ must be applied to the daily acts of sin, which break

our fellowship with God. This brings release from the road-blocks that are thrown up when we try to pray to God.

But this forgiveness is conditional. "If we confess our sins, he is faithful and just and will forgive us our sins and purify us from all unrighteousness" (1 John 1:9). If we want continued cleansing from the things we do day by day that ruin our fellowship with God, we must agree that what we have done is sin and ask him to forgive us. When we do this, our fellowship with God is restored.

Forgiven/Forgive

Confession of sin is the basis for our vertical forgiveness from God. But how does this impact our horizontal forgiveness of others? And for our purposes here, what impact does it have on God answering our prayers?

If we enjoy the benefits of salvation, we of all people ought to be forgiving. That's what Jesus was driving at in Matthew 6:12–15 and in the parable of the unmerciful servant in Matthew 18:21–35. This would be a good time to set this book aside and read that parable. It deals very clearly with the issue of forgiven/forgive.

When we who are forgiven by God forgive others, two things happen. First, we pray to God and *unconditionally release* to him the hurt of someone's unkind word or deed. It isn't ours anymore; we have given it to God without condition. Jesus said, "And when you stand praying, if you hold anything against anyone, forgive him, so that your Father in heaven may forgive you your sins" (Mark 11:25).

This is called "vertical forgiveness" by Wendell Miller because it is between God and each of us alone. It is when we unconditionally release the penalty of the offense to God. The offense against us is now in heavenly hands; we never need consider retaliation when the offense is no longer in our hands. That's a freeing experience.

Second, after we have released the offense to God, we are now free to release the offender from the offense. This "horizontal forgiveness" is more difficult because it is largely beyond our control. In addition, it is conditional. Again, Jesus is our authority. "If your brother sins, rebuke him, and if he repents, forgive him" (Luke 17:3).

We can only release our brother from the alienation that his sin has caused if he is willing to repent of that sin. We are held hostage to the offender's willingness to repent. We can forgive his offense because that is between God and us, but we can only forgive the offender when he or she has met God's conditions.

Do what God requires when you have been hurt. Commit that hurt to God in prayer and leave it there. Talk with the person who has hurt you, and give opportunity for repentance. If that repentance does not come, you have done all God has asked of you. If repentance does come, forgive and rejoice. Your brother and you have done all God requires of you both, and your prayer line to heaven is secure.

No Forgiveness/No Answer

What happens if we choose not to forgive others? Will we forfeit our salvation? No, that's impossible. It was God's gift to us and is neither returnable nor forfeitable. Failure to forgive others has no effect on our positional righteousness. Once justified, we remain justified forever.

However, our fellowship with our heavenly Father will be hampered. Our relationship with the only one who can answer our prayers will be dampened. What's more, harboring an unforgiving spirit will deter God from answering when we pray.

Years ago Lutheran theologian Richard C. H. Lenski wrote, "It is most vital for acceptable prayer that the petitioner forgive all his fellow men. Let us not delude ourselves that we are most firmly believing and filling our prayers with faith while secretly, in our hearts, we hold something against somebody."[29]

If you have an unforgiving spirit, don't expect much from your prayers. The only prayer that is effective when you have been hurt by someone is the prayer that commits that hurt to God and releases the offender from the consequence of it.

What's a Person to Do?

You don't want God to turn a deaf ear to your prayers, and yet you know holding an unforgiving grudge against someone is a significant prayer blocker. What should you do if you need to forgive someone?

Imbibe the spirit of forgiven/forgive. Admit that it is incumbent upon you, having been forgiven by God, to be forgiving to others. It's not a nice thing you should do—it's the command of God. If you fail to imbibe the forgiven/forgive spirit, don't read any further. Answered prayer is not in your future.

Take an honest inventory of your own forgiveness needs. Do as the old song says about Santa Claus—make a list and check it twice. List what you've done that's naughty and nice. Be honest. Don't pad that nice stuff and scrimp on the naughty stuff. Take an honest inventory of all the things in your life that need to be forgiven by others. When you and I admit that we aren't the saints our mothers think we are, we'll be more apt to be forgiving with others.

Seek God's forgiveness. Our greatest need for forgiveness is from God. Apply the 1 John 1:9 principle to your life. Get a clean bill of health from God before you start cleaning up your records with others. If you're not certain you have been forgiven by God, you'll not be inclined to forgive anyone else.

Seek an opportunity to grant forgiveness. Most of us have the "They hurt me; they'd better come to me and make it right" attitude about forgiveness. But Jesus never sat back and waited for sinners to come to him. He always sought them out, and in the process, he was frequently asked to grant forgiveness. If you are more like Christ, you will seek more opportunities to forgive.

When the opportunity comes, forgive and pray. When your wife asks to be forgiven for a short temper around the house, be gentle and understanding of the pressures of running a household. Be forgiving. When your husband asks to be forgiven for not being as attentive to you as he should be, be gentle and understanding of the sympathetic differences between men and women. Be forgiving.

When forgiveness precedes prayer, answers follow. When it doesn't, roadblocks to prayer result. Remove the prayer blockers. Return to forgiven/forgive fellowship with those around you. You may be surprised at how wide this opens the door for answered prayer.

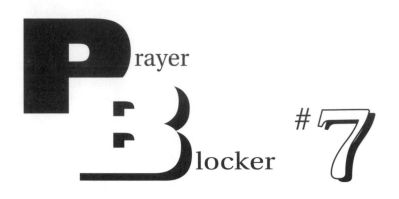

Prayer Blocker #7

God doesn't answer when

We Ask with the Wrong Motives

Man sees your actions, but God your motives.
                                        Thomas à Kempis

You've checked your life against the principles of God's Word. You've confessed your sin and are ready to pray. Your relationship with God seems to be good. You're all set.

You go to your room and get down on your knees. After pouring your heart out to God, you rise expectantly. You're convinced God will answer your prayer. But he doesn't. God is still silent. What's wrong? What could possibly be keeping him from answering your prayers?

Maybe something is wrong with your reasons for praying. Perhaps your motives aren't what God deems acceptable and it's time for a motives tune-up. Praying with the wrong motives is as fruitless as praying with unconfessed sin or an unforgiving spirit.

Karen was a Christian teenager living in a small Midwest community. Her dad and mom worked hard so they could afford to send Karen to a Christian school. Like any teen, Karen had her ups and downs. Most of the time she enjoyed school and was an important part of the church youth group. But Karen had a wild side. None of the Christian guys caught her eye. In fact, more often than not, Karen dated the unsaved guys at the city high school.

Karen knew her folks loved her. Often they prayed with her about school, church, boyfriends—all things important to Karen. She assured them everything was okay, but she knew it wasn't.

In the spring, Karen began to date Todd. A Prince Charming Todd was not, but he had a larcenous attitude toward life, and Karen liked that. Her parents did not approve of Todd, so Karen asked God to change their minds. She pleaded, "Please God, make Mom and Dad like Todd. They're so suspicious of him. If they'd only give him a chance. They've just gotta like Todd. I really want this, God. If they like Todd maybe they'll get off my back. You gotta make it happen, Lord. I know you can do it!"

But God didn't do it. Karen started cutting classes at school to be with Todd. She began to make excuses why the youth group had nothing to offer anymore. Karen's mother and father could see the infectious influence Todd had on her life. Finally there was a blowup. Her parents told Karen she couldn't see Todd anymore. Karen's sarcastic response: "Thanks a lot, God. Glad you came through for me."

Motive Is the Key

Have you ever felt like Karen? Maybe you've prayed earnestly and been surprised when God didn't come through for you. Perhaps Karen's problems are your problems too.

Often we pray with motives that are no better than Karen's "maybe they'll get off my back" motive.

Motive is the reason why we do what we do. Our actions are open and public; our motives are frequently secret and hidden.

Lucy holds the football for Charlie Brown. She promises this time he'll kick it a mile. "Let me help you build your confidence, Charlie Brown." But if you have enjoyed the Peanuts gang for decades, you are painfully aware of Lucy's secret motivation. Once again, she humiliates the round-headed kicker when she pulls the football away and he falls flat on his back.

Sometimes God does not answer our prayers because of the reasons why we pray. If those reasons are unwholesome, selfish, petty, or prideful, God does not view himself under any obligation even to consider them. What common motivation causes God to ignore our prayers? Asked another way, what is it in our heart that keeps God from answering our prayers?

No Secret Motives

Is it possible God knows my innermost secrets and hidden motives? Our motivation may be buried deep within us, but that does not stop God from reading us like a book and responding to us out of his holiness. The Bible says: "You have set our iniquities before you, our secret sins in the light of your presence" (Ps. 90:8). "For God will bring every deed into judgment, including every hidden thing, whether it is good or evil" (Eccles. 12:14). "He reveals deep and hidden things; he knows what lies in darkness, and light dwells with him" (Dan. 2:22). Jesus said, "Your Father, who sees what is done in secret, will reward you" (Matt. 6:4, 6, 18). "For there is nothing hidden that will not be disclosed, and nothing concealed that will not be known or brought out into the open" (Luke 8:17). "Nothing in all creation is hidden from

God's sight. Everything is uncovered and laid bare before the eyes of him to whom we must give account" (Heb. 4:13).

While it is possible to hide why we do what we do from our children, our neighbors, our parents, or our pastor, it is impossible to hide our motives from God. No prayer powered by petty motivation will move the heart of God.

Sometimes we think our prayers are properly motivated and God still does not answer them. The reason may be that our minds deceive us. "The heart [seat of emotions] is deceitful above all things and beyond cure. Who can understand it?" (Jer. 17:9). We simply do not understand what's in our heart the way God does. C. S. Lewis wrote, "Humans are very seldom either totally sincere or totally hypocritical. Their moods change, their motives are mixed, and they are often themselves quite mistaken as to what their motives are."[30] While it's difficult for us to know our motives, it's not difficult for God to know them.

Selfish Motives

Is it wrong for you to pray for yourself? Not at all. If praying for yourself is wrong, Moses was wrong (Exod. 33:18), Hannah was wrong (1 Sam. 1:11), David was wrong (2 Sam. 24:10–25), Solomon was wrong (1 Kings 3:7–9), Jabez was wrong (1 Chron. 4:10), Jonah was wrong (Jonah 2:1–10), Paul was wrong (Rom. 1:10), even Jesus was wrong (Matt. 26:39–42). But they were not wrong.

The Savior bids us to ask for what we need. He said, "Ask and it will be given to you" (Matt. 7:7). Jesus taught us to pray, "Give us today our daily bread" (Matt. 6:11). Jesus used the analogy of earthly parents delighting in giving to their children to illustrate that our heavenly Father desires to give us what we want as well (Matt. 7:11). Praying for our desires is not selfish as long as our desires are not selfish.

Praying for ourselves and our personal needs is both legitimate and encouraged in Scripture (see e.g., John 11:22;

15:16; Eph. 3:20; James 1:5; 1 John 3:22; 5:14–15). It's not personal prayer that God turns a deaf ear to, it's selfish prayer.

Selfish prayer is prayer that puts our interests ahead of God's interests or the interests of others. Warren Wiersbe says, "God enjoys answering prayer and meeting our needs. Selfish praying, however, is not the same as praying for ourselves. We pray for ourselves that we might be able to serve others. We pray for our needs that we might be able to meet the needs of others."[31]

When we pray selfishly, we pray that God will meet a need that benefits no one but ourselves, and may even harm others. Selfish prayer has a one-directional focus—inward. Selfishly motivated prayer never takes God's glory into consideration nor another's good. That's what makes it selfish.

One day Jesus was teaching the multitudes. He warned them against hypocrisy explaining that "there is nothing concealed that will not be disclosed, or hidden that will not be made known" (Luke 12:2). Suddenly someone in the crowd, who apparently wasn't paying much attention to what Jesus said, blurted out, "Teacher, tell my brother to divide the inheritance with me" (v. 13). Talk about something coming out of left field! This had nothing to do with Jesus' subject, but the man's anger had apparently been churning in his mind, and he wanted Jesus to settle a family dispute.

The man's remarks betrayed a selfish motivation. He cared nothing for the glory of God, the plight of the poor, or the good of the people. His only concern was himself. Perhaps he had a legitimate gripe against his brother, but his pleading did not mask his motives. Jesus saw right through him and immediately related a parable about the harmful effects of greed.

Jesus told them of a rich man who planned to tear down his barns and build bigger ones because his grain crop was so abundant. The rich farmer said to himself, "You have plenty of good things laid up for many years. Take life easy; eat, drink and be merry" (Luke 12:19).

Jesus did not tell this parable to condemn hard work. He condemned the selfish attitude of a farmer who never once considered anyone but himself. "This is how it will be with anyone who stores up things for himself but is not rich toward God" (v. 21). The Almighty is never pleased with selfish prayer. Don't expect an answer if you pray selfishly.

Pleasure-Seeking Motives

Closely akin to praying selfish prayers is praying for our own pleasure. This motive leads us to pray for something we want just because we want it.

If you have raised children, you have surely encountered this logic before. You ask a two-year-old why he wants a candy bar, and he mumbles, "Because I want it." It's hard to argue with that logic. He wants it because he wants it. It brings pleasure to him, and that's reason enough to ask.

The classic Bible passage that relates to motives speaks directly to this issue. James implores his readers to quit quarreling and fighting among themselves and submit to God instead. He says,

> You want something but don't get it. You kill and covet, but you cannot have what you want. You quarrel and fight. You do not have, because you do not ask God. When you ask, you do not receive, because you ask with wrong motives, that you may spend what you get on your pleasures.
> James 4:2–3

There can be no clearer expression of the reason for unanswered prayer. You ask and do not receive because you ask with wrong motives. Your motivation is to spend whatever it is you ask for on your own pleasures. This is more than a selfish motivation, it's a spendthrift motivation. It's being a personal prodigal with God's answer to your prayer. Little wonder God is quiet when we pray with such motivation.

Hedonistic Motives

The King James Version translation of James 4:2–3 uses the word *lust:* "Ye lust, and have not. . . . Ye ask amiss, that ye may consume it upon your lusts." That's not a bad translation. Lust is anything for which we have a strong desire. James chose the word *hedone* in Greek for this idea. You don't have to be a rocket scientist to see a close English derivative: *hedonism,* the belief that pleasure or happiness is the sole goal of life. I have seen beach resorts that could be called "Club Hedonism," because they gladly accept their patrons' money for any form of pleasure they desire.

Praying for God to give you something for no greater purpose than your hedonistic pleasure is a sure way to have your prayers fall on deaf ears. Your motive must be higher than this if God is to answer your prayer.

Higher Motives Needed

How often I have heard wives pray, "Oh God, please change my husband. Make him easier to live with." While that prayer may bring a worthy result, it reflects an inward attitude of selfishness. The wife is not interested in God changing her husband for his benefit or for God's glory, she is only interested in God making life easier for her.

Perhaps you may need to pray for God to change your husband. He may not be a Christian and desperately needs an eternal change. But make the basis of your prayer your husband's eternal salvation, not your temporal comfort.

Pray that your husband will be saved for God's glory. Pray that God will change him to make your husband a useful servant to the Lord Jesus. Pray that God will bring peace to your home as a testimony to God's amazing grace. But do not allow your motive in praying for your husband to be anything less than an authentic concern for him. Make your prayer for his benefit, not for yours. That's the kind of un-selfish prayer God will answer.

What Motive Is Proper?

God simply isn't interested in hearing from us out of self-ish or hedonistic desires. These are improperly motivated requests. Improper motivation is praying for a new luxury Lexus when you know it means taking your children out of a Christian school to pay for it. Improper motivation is pray-ing that God will move you up the corporate ladder even though it means moving someone else out. Improper mo-tivation is praying that God will make you saleswoman of the year because you don't want your closest rival to receive the honor.

You wouldn't enter the presence of a president or monarch with such requests; why trivialize your audience with the sovereign God? It doesn't make sense, and yet it happens all the time.

There is one way to make sure you are praying with right motives. Pray this way: "Holy Father, grant to me only those things I request that bring glory to you and good to others and me." Pretty simple, isn't it? But good to others and us and glory to God are the only motivations that a holy God considers prayer worthy.

God's Glory or Mine?

There are lots of requests made every day by well-meaning people, but they are self-serving requests. "Lord, I need this new client. Make sure he chooses our firm." Sounds innocent enough. Jesus told us to ask and we would receive. But what in that request gives glory to God? Do we want the new client to impress our boss? Do we want this client so we can get a nice fat bonus? What is the motivation behind our request?

Here's an even more thorny kind of motivation. Your pastor prays, "O Lord, please help our church to grow." Surely we can't fault a pastor for that request. After all, the Jerusalem church grew by leaps and bounds. Do we think that happened without the benefit of prayer? Certainly church growth is always a proper prayer request. However, if the pastor's motivation is to become the next denominational or fellowship superstar, if he wants to be invited to speak at the next conference, if he wants everybody in town buzzing about his big church, if he wants the reporters and television newspeople there weekly for each new achievement, his motivation is improper.

The only true way to judge motivation is the glory factor. Will what we ask of God bring glory to him or to us? The *Westminster Shorter Catechism* begins with the question "What is the chief end of man?" and gives the answer "Man's chief end is to glorify God and to enjoy him forever."

If your purpose in prayer is not to glorify God and to enjoy him forever, you have run headlong into a huge prayer blocker. Any motivation other than this must be removed if you are to receive God's answer to your prayers.

What's a Person to Do?

The motivation issue is not as easy to assess as others, and therefore, you may be tempted to sidestep it. Resist that temptation. If your motivation is wrong, your service is wrong. If your motivation is wrong, your ministry is wrong. If your motivation is wrong, your prayers are wrong.

Here's what the Bible says you should do:

Begin with a serious motivation check. Do an honest appraisal of your motives. How will you do that? Swallow hard. This won't be easy. Ask your spouse, your fellow worker, or your closest friend for an honest assessment of how he or she reads your motivation. If that doesn't work, ask your children.

Remember what God said in Proverbs: "A friend loves at all times, and a brother is born for adversity" (17:17). "Wounds from a friend can be trusted" (27:6). "Perfume and incense bring joy to the heart, and the pleasantness of one's friend springs from his earnest counsel" (27:9). "As iron sharpens iron, so one man sharpens another" (27:17).

Only you can know your true motivation, but others have a keen sense of your motivation in the way you conduct your life. Seek godly counsel on checking your present motivation.

Search the Word for advice, clues, counsel, and examples of motivation that please God. Look for men and women whose prayer motivation was for God's glory, not for their own. Take King Hezekiah, for example. Surrounded by 185,000 Assyrian soldiers and facing certain annihilation, Hezekiah prayed earnestly to God. His motivation was evident in his request. "Now, O LORD our God, deliver us from his hand, so that all kingdoms on earth may know that you alone, O LORD, are God" (2 Kings 19:19).

That's being motivated by the glory of God. If you search the Scriptures to look for examples of such proper motivation, you'll be amazed at something that is happening while you search. You'll see your motivation beginning to change as a result of your time and interest in God's Word. It's amazing, but it happens. Let it happen to you.

If your prayers don't seem to be getting through to God, maybe the problem is the reason you offer them. Do a motivation check and leave in the dust every selfish purpose. It's one way to get answers to your prayers.

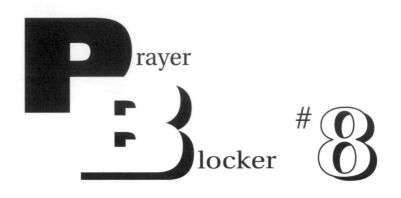

Prayer Blocker #8

God doesn't answer when

We Ask for the Wrong Things

Do not pray for easy lives. Pray to be stronger men. Do not pray for tasks equal to your powers. Pray for powers equal to your tasks.

Phillips Brooks

Let's face it. When God refuses to answer our prayers, it's not always because we are harboring sin in our lives or have an unforgiving spirit. There could be a much less sinister reason.

Sometimes it's not our motivation that's the problem in getting prayer answered; it's our requests. We simply ask for the wrong things. We make requests of God that there's no way he will answer. We have to admit it—God does not answer prayers that ask for the wrong things, even if we ask for the right reasons.

Many times this happens to us. We make what we think is a legitimate request of God. We wait for an answer, and the answer does not come. We go through a mental checklist of what might be the problem. What could be keeping

God from answering our prayer? Suddenly, there it is, right before our eyes. God didn't answer us because we made the wrong request.

Let's think about some requests that may fall on deaf ears in heaven. Likely you'll find similarities between these flawed requests and ones you have made. If you are puzzled why God hasn't answered your prayer, perhaps the pieces are about to fall together for you.

Prayers Contradictory to His Nature

God is sovereign. That means he can do anything, right? Not so fast. God is more than sovereign, he is also righteous, holy, compassionate, eminently fair, and just. One attribute of God will not overrule the others. That would make him a rather lopsided deity.

The wonder of God's character is that all his attributes glisten together as the multiple facets of a diamond. They present a brilliant, full-faceted God who is altogether lovely. Therefore, you should not expect God's love for the sinner to annul his anger at sin. God did not love the world so much that he simply looked the other way when we sinned. His love sent his Son to Calvary to pay the penalty for that sin and appease divine wrath. God balanced one attribute with the other.

In light of this, praying for something that is contrary to the very nature of God is like whistling in the dark. It may make you feel better, but it doesn't change anything. God will not answer a request that is contradictory to his divine nature.

Your city council frequently passes ordinances that appear to be anti-Christian. You have been advised to throw your hat into the ring and run for a seat on the council. That's the best way to have your voice heard. But in the process of campaigning, you learn that your staff has spread innuendoes about the other candidates to paint them in a bad light and increase your chances of getting elected. You know the rumors are probably not true, but you pray that God will use them anyway to discredit your opponents. You reason that because you are pro-life, pro-family, and pro-morality you deserve to win, and God will be pleased when you do.

Will God answer your prayers? I don't think so. Praying that his sense of moral justice will override his sense of fairness will never work. God's attributes balance one another; they do not contradict one another. God will not answer such a prayer because we ask for the wrong thing.

Prayers for Things Forbidden

God's Word is much more than a rule book; it is more like a guidebook. The Bible guides us toward eternity and gives us a road map to use every day on our journey. Sure, there are some dos and don'ts in the Bible. Any good guidebook will have them. We don't want to take a wrong turn. But it is an unfair oversimplification to say that the Bible is just a book of dos and don'ts.

The Bible is the revelation of the mind of God to the minds of men and women. It is a written record of what God wants us to know to live in peace and godliness. By following God's guidelines, we can live a life thoroughly pleasing to him and completely rewarding to us. When God says no in his Word, we can be certain there is a good reason. God wants our lives to be enjoyable, and every divine prohibition is to support the joy he has designed for us.

What happens when we disobey God? What happens when God prohibits something and we choose to disregard his wishes? Then we diminish our own joy and make our life less than it could be. Moses is a good example.

Raised in the posh extravagance of Pharaoh's palace, Moses allowed his emotions to get the best of him. He killed an Egyptian who was beating a Hebrew (Exod. 2:12) and spent the next forty years in Midianite oblivion. He thought his life was over. But God was merciful to him. He called to the reluctant shepherd from a burning bush (Exod. 3:1–10) and sent him back to Egypt to rescue the Hebrew people. The challenge of standing before the most powerful man alive and boldly demanding, "Let my people go," must have been a real heart-pounder. Seeing the waters of the Red Sea part to allow safe crossing for the Hebrews (Exod. 14:21–22) had to have been an emotional rush for Moses. And even though Moses' people were a grumbling bunch, to see God provide water, manna, quail, and all the Hebrews needed for their journey must have been an encouragement to this much-maligned leader.

When the Hebrew travelers finally arrived at Kadesh and found no water there, God told Moses, "Take the staff, and you and your brother Aaron gather the assembly together. Speak to that rock before their eyes and it will pour out its water" (Num. 20:8). We all know the story. Moses was emotionally overwhelmed at this point with the constant rebellion of the people. Instead of speaking to the rock as God had commanded, he raised his arm and struck it twice in frustration and anger (Num. 20:11).

God's response to Moses' disobedience was swift and final. He said to Moses, "Because you did not trust in me enough to honor me as holy in the sight of the Israelites, you will not bring this community into the land I give them" (Num. 20:12). The severity of God's punishment on Moses has been debated for generations, but the debate does not change the outcome. God would not permit Moses to enter the Promised Land.

However, this did not stop Moses from making one last shot-in-the-dark prayer asking God to change his mind. Deuteronomy 3:24–25 records Moses' unanswered prayer.

O Sovereign LORD, you have begun to show to your servant your greatness and your strong hand. For what god is there in heaven or on earth who can do the deeds and mighty works you do? Let me go over and see the good land beyond the Jordan—that fine hill country and Lebanon.

Moses had successfully negotiated with God before (Exod. 32:7–14); maybe it would work again. He began his prayer by extolling the sovereign God, the God who could do anything—even reverse his decision about forbidding Moses to enter the Promised Land. To Moses' prayer God responded, "Nothing doing!" Moses prayed for what God clearly had forbidden, and God would not answer that prayer.

Praying for God to bless your sin is useless praying. I received a letter a few years ago from a radio listener in California who had decided to leave her husband and marry another man in the church. She told me this man was more spiritual than her husband and would make a better choice as a life's mate. She was praying for God to work out the details. But her actions were carnally motivated and biblically unfounded. God does not answer prayers that request what he clearly has forbidden.

Prayers Contrary to His Program

When reading the Old and New Testaments, even a fledgling Bible student quickly becomes impressed that God has a program. That program was conceived before time began and will continue long after time is gone. It is an eternal program, formulated in eternity past, followed in eternity present, and fulfilled only in eternity future. Everything in God's program is happening exactly as he programmed it and is right on schedule.

Since we are frequently ignorant of God's program, either because he hasn't shared it with us or because we read his guidebook so infrequently that we don't know it, occasionally we pray for things that are not part of his eternal program. Somehow we expect God to change both time and eternity to accommodate our uninformed prayers. He won't do it. Our prayers go unanswered.

The mother of James and John came to Jesus one day and asked a favor. "Grant that one of these two sons of mine may sit at your right and the other at your left in your kingdom" (Matt. 20:21). Initially you may think that Mary's motivation was improper. How dare she take advantage of a family relationship to ask Jesus such a favor! But the text says nothing about her motivation, only her request. In fact, she knelt in worship before Jesus. That indicates her reverence for him. We cannot judge her motives, but we can certainly read Jesus' response: "You don't know what you are asking. . . . Can you drink the cup I am going to drink?" (Matt. 20:22).

Apparently James and John thought they could endure all that Jesus would endure, so the Savior responded, "You will indeed drink from my cup, but to sit at my right or left is not for me to grant. These places belong to those for whom they have been prepared by my Father" (v. 23). Translation: Don't ask for something contrary to the program of God. The places at Jesus' right or left hand belong to those whom God has prepared to take them.

Have you ever heard someone pray that God immediately stop all wars, end all of man's atrocities, cure all diseases, or end world hunger? While we all would like to see this happen, and some day it will, we also know that these evils are the result of sin and will not be removed until sin is ultimately removed.

God does not answer prayers requesting that he change his eternal program. It just won't happen. Such prayers are for the wrong things and fall on divine deaf ears.

Mutually Exclusive Prayers

This is what Harold Lindsell, in his book *When You Pray,* calls the law of internal contradiction. It is when we pray for two things, in Lindsell's words, "one of which it is not possible for God to say 'yes' to without saying 'no' to the other. In effect we are praying against ourselves. We do not even know that the one request is opposed to the other."[32] Perhaps an example of such a prayer will be helpful.

More than two decades ago I had a young student who had quite a testimony for the Lord. She was in Bible college preparing for whatever ministry the Lord had for her.

One day after class Kathy came to me for clarification about something I had said. During our conversation, she began quite spontaneously sharing the circumstances God used to bring her to himself. Kathy's parents were Christians. They served in various capacities in a church in New York State. But Kathy was wild and reckless. She wanted nothing to do with God, nothing to do with church, in fact, nothing to do with her parents.

After graduating from high school, Kathy packed what she could in a small bag and told her parents she was leaving home because she needed to find herself. By her own admission, Kathy was running away from God. Her parents knew what she was doing, and they asked two things of God: that he would save Kathy's soul and keep her from running away from home. What they didn't know was that, in the plan of God, their multiple requests were mutually exclusive.

Kathy ended up in Southern California. There she heard the message of the gospel, surrendered her life to Christ, and was wonderfully saved. There Kathy met Jesus Christ. There she had her divine appointment with destiny. Kathy told me, "I was running away from God, and I ran smack into Jesus."

Today Kathy is a lovely wife and mother. Her parents' prayers were only partially answered. They prayed that God would stop Kathy from running away from home and save her. God saved her, but she had to run away from home to run into Jesus. While Kathy's parents couldn't understand why God didn't keep their daughter from leaving home, now in retrospect they see that their requests could not both be answered as part of God's plan.

If you pray multiple requests to God and he doesn't answer them, perhaps it's because your multiple requests are mutually exclusive. Sometimes God cannot answer yes to one part of your prayer without answering no to another part. Just be grateful his wisdom is greater than your prayers.

Less than Best Prayers

One of the most delightful reasons God does not answer our prayers is because he has more to give us than what we request. If he were to give us what we ask for, we would be denied the better things he had intended to give us. Given that scenario, I'll take no for an answer anytime.

In his Sermon on the Mount, Jesus counseled us, "Ask and it will be given to you; seek and you will find; knock and the door will be opened to you" (Matt. 7:7). He then continued to ask some uncommon questions. "Which of you, if his son asks for bread, will give him a stone? Or if he asks for a fish, will give him a snake?" (vv. 9–10). When Luke records these questions he adds, "Or if he asks for an egg, will give him a scorpion?" (Luke 11:12).

The point is that God loves us even more dearly than our earthly father, and he will not give us what is not good for us. Asking good from the hand of God will never result in receiving bad from him. But asking good may result in not receiving the best. We should never allow that which is good to rob us of that which is best.

Elijah is a case in point. After his stunning victory on Mount Carmel against the prophets of Baal, Elijah prayed that God would return the rain that had been so noticeably absent for three and a half years. While praying, seven times Elijah sent his servant to look toward the Mediterranean for any sign of a shower. Six times the servant saw nothing, but on the seventh he reported, "A cloud as small as a man's hand is rising from the sea" (1 Kings 18:44). There it was. God had miraculously answered Elijah's fervent prayer. Yet after the thrill of these victories, the prophet would experience the agony of his most humiliating defeat.

Elijah fled to Mount Horeb as a result of threats on his life by wicked Queen Jezebel (1 Kings 19:1–3). Arriving at Beer-sheba in the Negev desert, Elijah took refuge from the hot Middle Eastern sun under a scruffy tree. It wasn't much protection. His situation seemed hopeless. If Jezebel's army caught up with him, it surely meant Elijah's death. If the prophet didn't find better shelter than this tree, it surely meant his death. Either way, Elijah was a dead man.

What do you do when your situation appears to be hopeless? You pray, but not as Elijah did. He prayed, "I have had enough, LORD. . . . Take my life; I am no better than my ancestors" (1 Kings 19:4). Elijah saw no way out. His life was over. He prayed for what he thought was good, but God had something much better in mind. After refusing to answer Elijah's prayer, God permitted the prophet to live approximately ten more years. What happened during that decade? Elijah had a personal encounter with God (1 Kings 19:12); he predicted the bloody demise of Ahab and Jezebel (1 Kings 21:17–23); and he transferred the mantle of his prophetic responsibilities to his understudy, Elisha (2 Kings 2:9–12).

Elijah prayed, "Take my life." God did not answer. Elijah was disappointed, but he would have been more disappointed if God had answered his prayer. Elijah's prayer was not answered because God had more for him to do. But there is an even more stunning reason for unanswered prayer. God had something better for him. Elijah and Elisha were walking together when "suddenly a chariot of fire and horses of fire appeared and separated the two of them, and Elijah went up to heaven in a whirlwind" (2 Kings 2:11). God refused to answer Elijah's prayer for death because, had he done so, Elijah would have missed the chariot of fire.

Aren't you glad God doesn't always answer your prayers? Your prayers are for your good; God's answers are for your best. Don't be disappointed when God doesn't answer. Maybe he has some chariots of fire in your future.

Asking for the wrong things is as ineffective as asking with the wrong motives. God will not answer your prayers when you make inappropriate requests.

What's a Person to Do?

How can you be sure you are asking for the right things? It's not as hard as you may think.

Look around you. What evidence do you see that God is answering the prayers of others in your church? Perhaps you should reconsider your requests if God is responding to their prayers and not to yours.

Look behind you. What evidence do you see that God has answered your prayers in the past? Have you changed your requests recently and found failure as a result? Change them again and ask for the right things.

Look within you. Double-check those motives one more time. Maybe your right motivation has slipped during times of successful praying. Review chapter 7 and make sure your motives are glorifying to God.

Above all, make sure your requests are grounded in God's Word, empowered by God's Spirit, and pleasing to God's Son. When we ask for the right things, we are more assured of a positive answer. The Bible paints a picture both of people who asked God for the right things and of people who asked him for the wrong things. Study these pictures, because they were painted for your instruction.

Ask the Spirit of God to guide you in the requests you make. After all, if he can take your innermost thoughts and convey them to God the Father, don't you think rooting out requests that displease God would be a big help in getting answers to your prayers?

Always use the "Does this please my Savior?" guideline when praying to God. Jesus is God's Son, and in him the Father is well pleased. What pleases the Son pleases the Father. Make requests that please the Son, and you won't have to worry about asking for the wrong things of the Father.

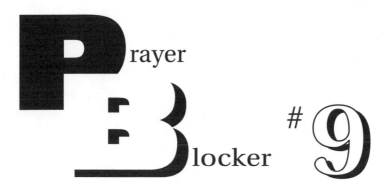

Prayer Blocker #9

God doesn't answer when

We Do Not Ask in God's Will

I was frustrated out of my mind, trying to figure out the will of God. I was doing everything but getting into the presence of God and asking Him to show me.

Paul Little

If you do the shopping in your home, do you make a shopping list before you go to the store? Probably you do, but does your list reflect your family's food tastes or what you enjoy cooking? Do you stack your list with your favorites? When you enter the portals of produce, are you armed with a self-devised, self-contained, and sometimes selfish list of things to buy? Maybe I should ask your family.

Think of this another way. When you visit the grocery store, do you buy things you need or things you like? Will your cart be loaded with what the kids badgered you for or things they really need? Will you cave in to impulsive buying and child coercion, or will you follow a higher standard? All of us succumb, at times, to the indelible memories of a cute commercial or a product jingle that we just can't get out of our head, but smart shoppers are not impulsive or bad-gered shoppers. Smart shoppers yield their will to real need.

Frequently the same is true in the way we pray. We go to God with a shopping list that doesn't really reflect anybody but us. Or we are badgered by others to pray for what they want instead of yielding our will to God's will in asking for what they need. Do you ever come away from prayer feeling that God's will was left unexpressed? Failure to pray for God's will is a sure and certain way of failing to have our prayers answered.

Laying the Foundation

We should not be surprised that God wants to answer our prayers. God is a giver by nature. In fact, he is a sacrificial giver. He gave his only begotten Son to be our Savior (John 3:16). How shall a God who did not spare his own Son fail to give us the good things we ask? (Rom. 8:32). A God who gives is a God who gives answers to prayer.

When Jesus arrived at the home of Lazarus, four days after his friend had died, Martha said, "Lord, . . . if you had been here, my brother would not have died. But I know that even now God will give you whatever you ask" (John 11:21–22). God the giver gives whatever Jesus asks. That's true for Jesus, but is it true for you?

A short time later Jesus said to his disciples, "My Father will give you whatever you ask in my name" (John 16:23). That's quite a promise! Of course there is a qualifier. We must ask in Jesus' name, that is, in the authority of Jesus' person. We may confidently ask anything of God because we boldly approach him through the merits of what Jesus did for us at Calvary (Heb. 4:14–16).

A classic Bible passage that addresses asking in prayer places another important qualifier on our receiving: "This is the confidence we have in approaching God: that if we ask anything according to his will, he hears us. And if we know that he hears us—whatever we ask—we know that we have what we asked of him" (1 John 5:14–15).

God always gave Jesus what he prayed for because Jesus always prayed for what he knew was the will of the Father. His prayer in the Garden makes this clear: "Father, if you are willing, take this cup from me; yet not my will, but yours be done" (Luke 22:42). But is it the same with us? Do we always pray for what we know is the Father's will? When we do, we have assurance that he hears us. "We know that God does not listen to sinners. He listens to the godly man who does his will" (John 9:31). When we disregard his will, we have no guarantee of the divine ear. When God doesn't answer, it may be because we have prayed for what we want but have not prayed for what God wants.

Pray Conditionally

If you always know God's will, you have insight the rest of us don't have. God's will is not always clear to most of us, and that can be a problem when we pray.

Certainly we know some things are God's will—things clearly stated in his Word. "It is God's will that you should be sanctified: that you should avoid sexual immorality; that each of you should learn to control his own body in a way that is holy and honorable" (1 Thess. 4:3–4). "Give thanks in all circumstances, for this is God's will for you in Christ Jesus" (1 Thess. 5:18). "For it is God's will that by doing good you should silence the ignorant talk of foolish men" (1 Peter 2:15). But not everything is as cut and dried as this.

That's why we must pray conditionally if we are to have our prayers answered. If you are not certain something is God's will, pray that he will answer in his will. James is instructive here. He said,

Now listen, you who say, "Today or tomorrow we will go to this or that city, spend a year there, carry on business and make money." Why, you do not even know what will happen tomorrow. What is your life? You are a mist that appears for a little while and then vanishes. Instead, you ought to say, "If it is the Lord's will, we will live and do this or that.

James 4:13–15

We live subject to the will of God *(Deo volente);* we should pray the same way. The great prayers of the Bible reflect this conditionality. Paul wrote to the Romans, "I pray that now at last by God's will the way may be opened for me to come to you" (Rom. 1:10). Later in that epistle he made a request of the Roman believers: "Pray that I may be rescued from the unbelievers in Judea and that my service in Jerusalem may be acceptable to the saints there, so that by God's will I may come to you with joy and together with you be refreshed" (Rom. 15:31–32). In both instances, notice how the apostle couched his prayer in the language of conditionality. He prayed for God's will.

Leave the Details to God

When we pray in God's will instead of our own, we are forced to leave the details of the answer to God. It's a good position to be in. Since we cannot make our prayers happen, we must rely on God to make them happen. He will do so in his own time and his own way. That's really praying in the right will.

Lindsell was right when he commented, "God reserves two decisions for himself in answering prayer. They are the decisions *when* and *how* prayer will be answered. . . . If we probe deeply, most of us find ourselves telling God exactly how we think he should answer our prayers and when he ought to do it. And if God does not do it our way we are annoyed."[33]

Wait a While

When should God answer our prayers? Most of us think he should answer immediately. One of the most unwelcome words in the English language is *wait*. Even *no* is sometimes easier to take than *wait*. But God often delays his answer for our good. He is not at all intimidated by our demand for instant gratification in prayer.

God sometimes delays his answer to allow us time to modify our requests so that they more closely conform to his will. After all, God wants to say yes to our requests. He only says no when there is reason to do so. If need be, God will delay so that we can sharpen the focus of our requests and bring them into compliance with his will.

Sometimes God delays his answer to cause us to drop an inappropriate request. He doesn't say no; he simply says nothing. He knows that once we have had time to think through our request, we will see how childish and inappropriate it is. God in his grace delays in order to allow us to grow up in him and ask for things that please him.

God sometimes delays his answer to build character in us. Kinko's, McDonald's, Polaroid, and Nescafé are all companies or products that have been built on the twentieth-century need for immediacy. We want copies made, and we want them right now. We're in such a hurry that we can't stop to eat, so we dash through the drive-thru and eat in our car as we steer one-handed down the highway. We can't wait a few days for our photos to be developed anymore, and when we want coffee, we want it instantly.

Much of business operates on the principle that immediate is best—but not the business of prayer. Character qualities such as patience, submission, endurance, understanding, and trust all require time to develop. Delayed prayer is one of God's beautiful classrooms for character development.

God sometimes delays his answer to test our faith. How do you respond when you pray and God does not answer immediately? Do you begin to question whether or not he will answer at all? Some people see God as little more than a cosmic Santa Claus. They shoot up a prayer request and if he doesn't instantly respond, they move on to another Santa in another department store. God is a loving, giving, caring Father who wants to answer our prayers. He simply chooses to answer only in concert with the timetable of his divine will. Waiting for God to answer proves we have faith that he will answer, in his time.

Second-Guessing God

Equally important to leaving the *when* to God is leaving the *how* to him. We all have our own preconceived ideas about how God will answer our requests. Sometimes, when his answers do not correspond to our ideas, we become angry at God. "How could he not see how much I needed this?" "Doesn't God understand that I need money for a whole year, not just one semester?" Second-guessing God is almost a national pastime for Christians.

What are some things you've prayed about recently that God did not answer as you expected? Did you ask him for better health, and instead your car broke down so you had to walk to work? Did you pray for more money to run your household, and instead you discovered a budget you had drawn up a year ago and never implemented? Paul prayed three times for his thorn in the flesh to be removed, and instead God gave him added grace to endure it (2 Cor. 12:8–9). God answers our prayers in his will as he wishes. We are better off to allow him the freedom of his will.

When and How

Joseph had a dream in which his brothers and he were binding sheaves of grain. Suddenly his sheaf stood upright while their sheaves gathered around and bowed down to it (Gen. 37:5–7). This was God's way of telling Joseph that his brothers would fall before him one day in obedience. But Joseph could never have guessed *when* and *how* God would fulfill that dream. He never surmised that his brothers would hate him enough to sell him to a passing camel caravan. He never guessed he would work for an Egyptian with a seductive wife or be thrown into an Egyptian dungeon. He certainly never dreamed he would one day become prime minister of Egypt. All of this was in the *when* and *how* of God, just the way the answers to our prayers are.

Earlier I related the story of a former student named Kathy who, in running away from God, ran into Jesus Christ. Her story is similar to that of Augustine, the great fourth-century church father. His mother, Monica, was concerned about her son's salvation. She learned Augustine was planning to leave home and go to Rome, a cesspool of iniquity. She pleaded with God that he not permit her son to go, but God did not answer this mother's well-motivated prayer. Divine will overrode a mother's will.

What Monica could not have known was that Augustine had to go to Rome because, in the eternal will of God, there he would encounter Ambrose, bishop of Milan, and through him come to trust Christ as Savior. God's will, done in God's way and in his time, is always best for us. Never complain about God being slow. He is just being deliberate.

What's a Person to Do?

If you want answers to your prayers, and you're not certain what you're praying for is God's will, do what others in your situation have done. Pray conditionally. Pray that God will answer you according to his will. And ask yourself these questions:

Will what I ask bring glory to God?

Will it be beneficial to other believers as well as to me?

Will my request bring any shame to the name of Christ?

Will it bring short-term pleasure but long-term sorrow?

Will what I ask help people or hinder them?

Will it help me to grow spiritually, to be a better witness?

Will this be the kind of request Jesus would make?

Will I be sorry at the judgment seat of Christ that I made this request?

If you ask anything in God's will, you won't have to worry about the answers to these and other probing questions. God will make the answers plain and your prayers acceptable.

Never worry about the *when* and *how* of answered prayer. These are beyond your control but well within the firm grasp of sovereign control—the control of God. If you can commit the *what* of your life to God's omnipotence, can't you trust the *when* and *how* to his omniscience?

Prayer Blocker #10

God doesn't answer when

We Are Hindered by Satanic Interference

A believer who overestimates Satan's power can live an entire lifetime in fear.... On the other hand, a person who underestimates the power and cunning of Satan may become unconcerned with Satan's activity and be lulled into complacency.

George Sweeting

Since prayer involves such a vital relationship with God, Satan is intent on blocking that relationship by any means possible. Usually it's quite easy. He entices us to harbor some hidden, menacing sin that hinders our prayer life. If that doesn't work, the devil incites conflict between our friends or family and us. When we treat each other badly, when we refuse to forgive offenses, Satan knows he has hamstrung our prayers.

What if all these prayer blockers fail? What if we have a handle on those things that keep us from being intimately related to God? What is left in Satan's bag of tricks to hinder our prayers and keep God from responding to us?

The answer is both simple and scary. Simply put, when Satan can't trust you to block your praying relationship with God, he does the job himself. That's the scary part. Satan will actually involve himself and his henchmen in disrupting your prayers. If he can't keep your prayers from getting through to God, he will do whatever is necessary to keep God's answer from getting through to you.

Impossible, you say? Think again. We now explore one of Satan's subtlest and evilest ways to keep God from answering your prayers—satanic interference.

Many who read the Bible avoid the prophetic books—especially Revelation and Daniel—because they think prophecy is too difficult to understand. But there are many lessons we can learn about life here and now in these apocalyptic writings. In fact, the Book of Daniel is our primary source for knowing how Satan personally gets involved in throwing up prayer blockers between your prayers and God's answers.

Daniel's Praying Relationship with God

When we first encounter Daniel in the book that bears his name, he is just a boy. We know little about him except that he was part of the royal family, the ancestors of Jesus Christ (Dan. 1:3–6). Even as a youth, Daniel had a very strong relationship with God. He lived a godly life under stressful conditions and refused to compromise his religious convictions (1:8).

From the testimony of his contemporary, the prophet Ezekiel, Daniel was known for his righteousness (Ezek. 14:14, 20) and his wisdom (Ezek. 28:3). He would grow to become a man not unlike Noah or Job. Daniel had a vibrant relationship with God.

But that relationship was severely tested when Daniel was carried into captivity by King Nebuchadnezzar and his Babylonian armies. Under the strain of emotional and spiritual pressure, however, Daniel's love and loyalty to God flourished.

Daniel and the Dream Team

Nebuchadnezzar had a dream about a warrior statue that troubled him greatly. His court astrologers said no one could interpret the dream unless it was revealed by the gods (2:11). Daniel asked his friends Shadrach, Meshach, and Abednego to pray with him that God would give him the interpretation of the dream. And God revealed it to him down to the last detail.

No one was more impressed than the king. He praised the God of heaven and fell prostrate before Daniel, honoring him (2:46–47). Nebuchadnezzar promoted the dream team— Shadrach, Meshach, and Abednego—to administrative positions in Babylon. Daniel served the king in the royal court.

Years later Nebuchadnezzar had another dream, this time about a gigantic tree. Again Daniel came to the rescue, but this time he had bad news for the king. Nebuchadnezzar would go mad. He would eat grass like the cattle, grow hair like the feathers of an eagle, and nails like the claws of a bird (4:24–25, 33). It wasn't a pretty picture. Although a man of significant pride (4:29–30), Nebuchadnezzar came to trust Daniel and "glorify the King of heaven, because everything he does is right and all his ways are just" (4:37).

The Elder Statesman

Nebuchadnezzar died after ruling Babylon for forty-three years, but Daniel's ministry to pagan kings went much further. Nebuchadnezzar was succeeded by his son Evil-Merodach, who reigned just two years (562–560 B.C.) and was murdered by his brother-in-law, Neriglissar. This man ruled four years (560–556 B.C.) and was succeeded by his young son, who was assassinated two months later by Nabonidus. Belshazzar, Nabonidus's eldest son, was appointed as coregent during his father's seventeen-year reign (556–539 B.C.). So when Daniel 5:2 speaks of Belshazzar as Nebuchadnezzar's son, it does so in the sense of descendant.

Belshazzar also needed Daniel's interpretive skills. At a great banquet, Belshazzar made the fatal mistake of drinking from the gold and silver goblets that Nebuchadnezzar had taken years earlier from the temple in Jerusalem. When human fingers began to write on the wall, Belshazzar nearly died of fright. Later that night he did die, after Daniel interpreted the handwriting on the wall (5:30). Darius the Mede then became king over Babylon. The year was 539 B.C.

Daniel had now lived in Babylonian captivity sixty-six years. He wasn't a teenager anymore; he was a distinguished, respected, elder statesman. Cyrus, king of Persia, decreed that all Babylonian exiles should return to their homelands. Thousands of Jews did, but not Daniel. When he received a revelation from God in the third year of Cyrus (perhaps 536 or 535 B.C.), Daniel was an old man (10:1–3). I never cease to be amazed how many years God will use people if they remain clean before him.

The Praying Prophet

What did the old prophet do when his final vision came from God? What he always did. "At that time I, Daniel, mourned for three weeks. I ate no choice food; no meat or wine touched my lips; and I used no lotions at all until the three weeks were over" (Dan. 10:2–3). These were the usual preparations for prayer. Although these verses do not actually say Daniel prayed, verse 12 makes it clear that he did. Daniel attempted to understand God's revelation by humbling himself and praying for wisdom.

Prayer was a significant part of the prophet's life. When Nebuchadnezzar dreamed of the warrior statue and determined to kill all his wise men because they could not decipher the dream, Daniel rushed to the dream team and asked them to get busy praying for wisdom. "He urged them to plead for mercy from the God of heaven concerning this mystery" (2:18).

Later, the decree that no one should pray to any god or man but Darius or risk being thrown into the lions' den was clearly aimed at Daniel. What would the prophet do? What he always did. He went to his upstairs window, got down on his knees, and prayed three times a day (6:10).

One day while reading the Scriptures, Daniel discovered that the Babylonian captivity was to last just seventy years. The prophet knew the time was almost up, so he fasted in sackcloth and ashes and offered his great prayer of Daniel 9. Daniel's relationship with God was energized three times a day by meaningful prayer. Daniel knew how to get answers from God.

An Answer from Heaven

Even for Daniel, however, answers to prayer were not always instantaneous. Daniel needed help in interpreting the vision of an impending war (10:1). He prayed, but no answer came. Daniel prayed some more. Surely God would honor his prayers. After all, he had done all the right things. Still nothing. Heaven was silent. Maybe you have also had this experience.

Daniel's mourning and fasting went on for three weeks. Had God forgotten him? Had he done something to offend God? The prophet was puzzled. Is there a greater puzzle in life than knowing you're right before God, knowing your requests are properly motivated, and still you get no answer from God? That was Daniel's dilemma. Why did God not answer his prayer?

An Angelic Answer

Suddenly, on the twenty-fourth day of the month, the elder statesman standing on the bank of the Tigris River looked up and saw God's answer. It was an angel. God had answered Daniel's prayer, and an angel was delivering the answer.

Heavenly visitors played more than bit parts in Daniel's drama. When Nebuchadnezzar revealed his tree dream, he said, "I looked, and there before me was a messenger, a holy one, coming down from heaven" (4:13). Nebuchadnezzar's nighttime visitor was an angel sent from God. That angel hinted at his job description when he said, "The decision is announced by messengers, the holy ones declare the verdict" (4:17). Daniel referred to the angel as "a messenger, a holy one, coming down from heaven" (4:23).

Angels are very prominent in Daniel's story. How did Daniel explain his safety in the lions' den? "My God sent his angel, and he shut the mouths of the lions" (6:22). When Daniel struggled to interpret the vision of the ram and the goat, the angel Gabriel was sent to reveal its meaning (8:16). Before Daniel concluded his prayer, Gabriel appeared and said, "Daniel, I have now come to give you insight and understanding. As soon as you began to pray, an answer was given, which I have come to tell you, for you are highly esteemed" (9:22–23). Before prayer was finished, God's answer was on the way.

An Angelic Appearance

Today there is a resurgence of interest in angels. Movies such as *Angels in the Outfield* and the television series *Touched by an Angel* are examples of this renewed interest. But much of our knowledge of angels is pure fiction. Daniel 10:5–6 gives us the most detailed description of an angel found anywhere in the Bible:

1. The angel appeared in the form of a man.
2. He was dressed in a linen garment, probably the dazzling white apparel referred to in Luke 24:4.
3. He wore a belt made out of the finest gold, perhaps in the form of chain links or gold embroidery.
4. His body glowed luminously like chrysolite, which is yellow topaz.
5. His face flashed like spectacular lightning.
6. His eyes blazed like bright torches (cf. Rev. 1:14).
7. The angel's arms and legs revealed the strength and splendor of burnished bronze.
8. His voiced thundered like the roar of the crowd at a stadium (cf. Rev. 10:1–3).

So forget the yellow wings, long blonde hair, and harp. Angels likely don't look much like medieval art or modern cinema.

Daniel had prayed for understanding to interpret God's vision. The Revealer of mysteries spared no effort to answer his prayer. God used a brilliant angel to deliver his answer personally to the praying prophet.

An Angelic Ministry

This angel did more than reveal God's secrets to Daniel. He ministered to Daniel's spirit as well. Those with Daniel were unable to see the angel, but they could sense his awesome presence, so they fled. Daniel was alone, face-to-face with an angel. His aging body couldn't take the excitement. His face turned deathly pale and he fainted (10:7–9).

The hand of the angel touched Daniel, and he recovered enough to rise to his hands and knees. The holy one said, "Stand up, for I have now been sent to you" (10:11). Daniel struggled to his feet and continued to tremble in stunned silence.

We shouldn't be surprised that an angel ministered to Daniel's physical needs. Hebrews 1:14 asks the question, "Are not all angels ministering spirits sent to serve those who will inherit salvation?" The angel was just doing what he was created to do—help people like Daniel, and you and me.

When you're waiting for God's answer and it's taking too long, it would be unbearable if it were not for the gracious encouragement of God's ministering spirits. This same angelic service is available to us. Accept the ministry of God's holy ones while you wait for your prayers to be answered.

An Outrageous Spiritual Conflict

The angel quieted Daniel's mind by saying, "Do not be afraid, Daniel. Since the first day that you set your mind to gain understanding and to humble yourself before your God, your words were heard, and I have come in response to them" (10:12). That's what Daniel was waiting for—confirmation that God had heard his prayer.

Daniel is very much like us. It had been three weeks since he began to pray for wisdom. What was taking God so long? If he hears and answers our prayers, why does it sometimes take weeks or even years for God to answer? Daniel must have been asking the same thing.

Suddenly the story takes a dark turn. Although God had heard Daniel's prayer three weeks earlier and had dispatched his holy angel with an immediate answer, the angel was intercepted by Satan. The angel explained, "But the prince of the Persian kingdom resisted me twenty-one days" (10:13). The prince of Persia is a poetic reference to a satanic secret agent sent to interfere with God's answer to Daniel's prayer. Satan had taken direct intervention to keep God's answer from getting through to Daniel.

The Cosmic Conflict

Don't be surprised. This kind of cosmic conflict has been going on since the day Satan rebelled against God (Ezek. 28:12–19). There have been some pretty significant skirmishes between Jehovah and Lucifer.

For us, the battle began in Eden's paradise (Gen. 3:1–6). It continued in the fraternal murder of Abel (Gen. 4:8). That the rebellion quickly spread to every human being is evident from God's assessment that "every inclination of the thoughts of his heart was only evil all the time" (Gen. 6:5).

Other notable satanic hostilities include:

the plot to kill Joseph, the only son who could keep the Patriarch's family alive (Gen. 37:18);

Saul's repeated attempts on the life of David (1 Sam. 19–29);

wicked Athaliah's slaughter of all the royal seed except Joash who was hidden by Jehosheba (2 Chron. 22:10–12);

Herod's murder of Bethlehem's infant boys two years of age and under (Matt. 2:16).

Satan's Waterloo came at the bloody battlefield called Calvary (Matt. 27:27–50), but he continues to attack. One day Lucifer will be cast into the lake of fire, and his long war against God will be over (Rev. 20:10). But until that day, the cosmic conflict continues to heat up.

The Nature of the Battle

Paul's parting words to the Ephesians could just as easily have been the angel's words to Daniel.

Put on the full armor of God so that you can take your stand against the devil's schemes. For our struggle is not against flesh and blood, but against the rulers, against the

authorities, against the powers of this dark world and against the spiritual forces of evil in the heavenly realms.
Ephesians 6:11–12

The battle hasn't changed much in thousands of years. Whether it's an angel being interfered with while carrying God's answer to prayer, a first-century Christian struggling against an evil world, or you and I being assaulted by an unseen foe, the enemy we face is very strong and deadly. But never forget that every satanic attack on God's people is in reality a heavenly battle fought on an earthly battlefield. We are not under attack—God is! Daniel didn't receive an answer to his prayer for three weeks, but it was God's answer, not Daniel's prayer, that was being interfered with.

When you pray but you don't receive God's answer, it could be that Satan is interfering. That's not always the case, of course, but it is sometimes the case. We dare not lightly dismiss satanic interference.

The Hidden Agenda

Satan's agenda only tangentially affects you and me. His target is God, not us. His agenda in interfering with our prayers is to destroy God's response, not our prayers. He doesn't want us to receive God's answer; he cares little about our request.

What is Satan's hidden agenda? William Cowper wrote, "Satan trembles when he sees the weakest saint upon his knees." The devil knows he cannot win the war, so he must settle for winning some skirmishes along the way. When we pray and our words wing their way to God, they enter enemy territory. Satan is the prince of the power of the air, the ruler of the kingdom of the air (Eph. 2:2). In order to reach the ears of God, our prayers pass through Satan's domain, and he doesn't like that.

If you ever have listened to a shortwave radio, you know how devastating interference can be when you're trying to receive a signal. Your patience runs thin when all you hear is static. Satan specializes in static. Satanic interference with your prayers is not just your imagination; it is real. Satan's three-week resistance to God's response when Daniel prayed proves it. Prayer is much more than petition to God; it is actual combat with Satan.

The devil knows that when he interferes with your prayers he interferes with your relationship to God. That's his agenda, and it's no longer hidden. If Satan can convince you that God didn't hear your prayer or that he doesn't care about your needs, that old devil knows he can chip away at your relationship with God. Don't let Satan use a delay in God's response as a tool to discourage you from praying. If you do, he wins and you lose.

Pray On

There's an old fable that says the devil once held a yard sale and offered all the tools of his trade to anyone who would pay his price. He spread them out on a table and labeled each one: hatred, malice, envy, despair, sickness, sensuality. They were all there, all the weapons Satan has used so skillfully in our lives. But off to one side lay a harmless looking instrument labeled "discouragement." Although it looked old and very worn, it was priced far above the rest. When asked why "discouragement" was priced so high, Satan replied, "Because it is so much more effective than the others. No one knows it belongs to me, so it's my greatest weapon."

If the delayed answer to Daniel's prayer teaches us anything, it teaches us that sometimes we are not the reason for God's silence, and neither is God. We can ask without faith and not receive a response. We can ask amiss and not receive a response. We can ask while harboring sin and not receive a response. And sometimes we can ask and God responds, but satanic interference keeps us from receiving that response. It has nothing to do with you or me. Satanic resistance alone prevents our prayers from being answered.

So pray on. If you have asked God to save your husband, pray on. If you have asked him to bring back your wayward child, pray on. If you are praying for grace to bear a seemingly unbearable hurt, pray on. Discouragement at not hearing God's response is the chief weapon in Satan's cosmic arsenal. You can defeat him if you pray on!

What's a Person to Do?

Daniel's story provides many opportunities for discouragement. The book opens with his young friends and him being uprooted from their homeland and carried into forced captivity by a bloodthirsty enemy. Soon there is the threat of death to all the wise men of Babylon, including Daniel and his friends. Then comes the fiery furnace fiasco, the handwriting on the wall, and the lions' den. No fun there. But the greatest source of discouragement had to be that Daniel prayed earnestly for three weeks and it seemed God wasn't interested enough to answer.

Is there anything in this story to encourage us? Does the Book of Daniel teach anything about anticipating answered prayer? Does it ever! Read those two little words at the end of Daniel 4:26: "Heaven rules."

When you pray and don't get the words quite right—heaven rules. When you pray and things are falling apart around you—heaven rules. When you pray and Satan interferes with God's answer—heaven rules.

Be encouraged when you pray. If you must wait weeks or even years for an answer, heaven rules. Satanic interference can never permanently block answers to your prayers. Some day, some glorious day, God will remove all the prayer blockers. The answer is on its way because *heaven rules!*

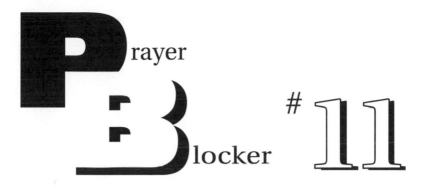

Prayer Blocker #11

God doesn't answer when

We Pray with Deniable Attitudes

Our attitude toward things is likely in the long run to be more important than the things themselves.

A. W. Tozer

There is an old African tribal saying: "The man who is not hungry says the coconut has a hard shell." Translation: Attitude is everything.

How skillfully we choose our words, how much experience we have, how eloquently we pray are not nearly as important to God as our attitudes about prayer. If we pray with deniable attitudes, it is unlikely that God will answer our prayers.

If God doesn't appear to be answering your prayers, check your attitudes. When the engine of your car doesn't fire up after you have turned the key, you immediately check the gauges on your dash. Do you have gasoline? Is the battery dead? These gauges are like attitude checks in your prayer life.

If prayer is not working for you, perhaps it's because you have some attitude deficiencies when you pray. Let's check

the gauges. We'll investigate ten of the most common attitudes that are important if we want God to hear and answer
our prayers.

The Attitude of Necessity

Ask people at church if prayer is necessary and almost
everyone will say that it is. Yet we treat prayer as if it were a
luxury instead of a necessity. A callous attitude toward prayer
is not likely to inspire God to answer our prayers.

Do you have any doubt that God has called us to pray?
Like worship and witness, prayer is the profession of the
Christian. Martin Luther said, "As it is the business of tailors
to make clothes, and cobblers to mend shoes, so it is the
business of Christians to pray." Prayer is what we Christians
do, just as teaching is what teachers do or plumbing is what
plumbers do.

But why is prayer necessary? What is it about prayer that
makes it essential? Two things: Prayer is God's will, and
prayer has no substitute.

If you want to know God's ways, read his Word. If you want
to know God's will, add prayer to reading your Bible. Prayer
is how we know God's will for our lives, and therefore, it *is*
God's will for our lives. It was Jesus' intent that we "should
always pray and not give up" (Luke 18:1). David entreated
God, "Let everyone who is godly pray to you while you may
be found" (Ps. 32:6). Samuel considered prayer so necessary
that he deemed failure to pray a sin (1 Sam. 12:23).

There is no substitute for prayer. Think about it. If you go
to a restaurant, you will likely find one or two sugar substi-
tutes on the table. There may also be a salt substitute. When
your server takes your order, you may ask if you can substitute something on the menu. We live in a substitute world.
But there is no substitute for prayer. If you do not talk to God

through prayer, you do not talk to God. Prayer is irreplaceable. Anything irreplaceable is necessary. If you go to God with the attitude that prayer is unnecessary, God may be inclined to think that answering your prayers is unnecessary as well.

The Attitude of Privilege

As a Bible teacher on an international radio broadcast, I have the privilege of teaching the Word and touching the world every day. It is a humbling and awesome responsibility that I do not take lightly. As an American, I have the privilege of living in a country where I may speak my mind, even about the things of God. As a resident of the State of Nebraska, I have the privilege of enrolling as a student at the University of Nebraska and receiving an education while watching the Nebraska Cornhuskers play some great football. These privileges come to me not because of my intrinsic worth but because of my status.

As a Christian, I also have certain privileges because of my status. I am born again, a joint-heir with Jesus, a child of the King. That secures for me many things, not the least of which is the opportunity to talk with God. Prayer is one of the great privileges of the Christian life. If we go to God with this attitude, God will be inclined to honor us with his response.

Why is prayer such a privilege? Three reasons come to mind immediately:

1. *Prayer is a privilege because of who is calling us to prayer.* We have an invitation to pray from almighty God himself. That makes prayer something akin to a command performance. None other than the sovereign God bids us to talk with him. "Call to me and I will answer you and tell you great and unsearchable things you do not know" (Jer. 33:3). How can we turn down an invitation like that?

2. *Prayer is a privilege because of the price Jesus Christ paid to give us access to God.* Prayer is not automatic. God doesn't always choose to hear or answer our prayers. But we would have no access to God at all had it not been for the atoning death of Jesus Christ on our behalf. Speaking of Jesus, the apostle Paul said, "Through whom we have gained access by faith" (Rom. 5:2). Access to whom? Access to the sovereign God. Access how? Access by faith. By what approach? By prayer. Paul repeats this theme in Ephesians 2:18 and 3:12. Accessing God only costs us some time and energy, but it cost our Savior his life. That's why we come to God with the attitude of privilege.

3. *When we pray we are not left to struggle by ourselves.* It is the privilege of a Christian to have an experienced and powerful Helper—the Holy Spirit. He does things for us when we pray that we couldn't possibly do for ourselves. "The Spirit helps us in our weakness. We do not know what we ought to pray for, but the Spirit himself intercedes for us" (Rom. 8:26).

As an American citizen I have had occasion to seek aid from the American embassy while traveling abroad. I can do so because I am an American; it is my privilege. But I have a greater privilege as a Christian. I can receive aid from the Spirit of God when I pray. Little wonder the attitude of privilege should accompany each of our prayers. Don't approach heaven without it.

The Attitude of Humility

A counterbalance to the attitude of privilege is the attitude of humility. Neither you nor I have an inherent right to enter the presence of God and petition him with our prayers. That right was forfeited by our sin. It was only regained when our sin was paid for, but you and I could not make that payment. The Lord Jesus made it for us when he "gave himself for us to redeem us from all wickedness" (Titus 2:14). We owe the privilege of prayer entirely to him. What a humbling thought.

Jonathan Edwards said, "Nothing sets a person so much out of the devil's reach as humility." That's true, but it is also true that humility sets a person close to God. Could it be that our failure to pray with humility is the reason for our failure to pray with power? Didn't God promise Israel, "If my people, who are called by my name, will humble themselves and pray . . . then will I hear from heaven" (2 Chron. 7:14)? Humility is always the ground for power.

But what does it mean to be humble? How do we pray with an attitude of humility? "Humility," says Henry Jacobsen, "is the ability to see ourselves as God describes us." The tax collector in Luke 18:10–14 did that. When he went to the temple to pray, he saw himself as God saw him—a simple sinner seeking a sovereign God. His humble view of himself enhanced his glorious view of God. Without lifting his head, the tax collector said, "God, have mercy on me, a sinner" (v. 13).

Contrast this with the Pharisee in the same parable. His proud view of himself detracted, in fact, prohibited his view of God. "The Pharisee stood up and prayed about himself" (v. 11). The difference in the attitudes of these two men made the difference in getting an answer to their prayers. Jesus made this practical application: "Everyone who exalts himself will be humbled, and he who humbles himself will be exalted" (Luke 18:14).

If we come to God with the attitude that he owes us an answer, we come with a deniable attitude. God can easily find just cause to refuse to answer us. Prayer is a privilege, but a humble privilege. It's a privilege you and I don't deserve, so we must pray as did the tax collector if we want our prayers answered. Pray with humility if you want to pray with power.

The Attitude of Earnestness

What is earnestness? Name one of your friends who is earnest. Can you define this attitude? Perhaps we should put it in St. Augustine's timely category: "I know what it is until you ask me."

Webster says earnestness is "characterized by or proceeding from an intense and serious state of mind."[34] God wants us to pray with earnestness—an intense and serious state of mind. Too much of our praying is perfunctory, even lackadaisical. Prayer that gets answered is prayer offered with earnestness. Our privilege that cost Jesus his life should not be approached with anything less than real seriousness.

Three different words are used in the New Testament that equate to *earnestness*. The first is found in Romans 8:19, "The creation waits in eager expectation," and Philippians 1:20, "I eagerly expect and hope that I will in no way be ashamed." The meaning is evident: Do everything with eager expectation of a response. That's how God wants us to pray, with eager expectation of his response.

The second word is used twice by Paul in 2 Corinthians 7. It means to yearn for something. In verse 7 the apostle says the Corinthians were "longing" for him in their deep sorrow. In verse 11 he says their sorrow had produced "earnestness" and "eagerness." They needed Paul, and they yearned for him to minister to them.

The third is the most common word and means to be more intense, to go above and beyond. For example, this Greek word *(perissoteros)* is used by Mark when he describes the angry crowd shouting all the louder, "Crucify him!" after Pilate questioned the guilt of Jesus (Mark 15:14). Paul used it of himself when describing his eagerness as a Pharisee: "I was advancing in Judaism beyond many Jews of my own age and was extremely zealous for the traditions of my fathers"

(Gal. 1:14). Paul used this word seven times in 2 Corinthians (1:12; 2:4; 7:13, 15; 11:23 [twice]; 12:15).

When we pray, God wants us to yearn for him, to eagerly expect his response, to go above and beyond in our conversation with him. Prayer is not a casual chat with God; it is much more. Prayer is an eager yearning for God. Donald G. Bloesch asks, "How can we be certain that God has in fact heeded our prayer . . . ? If we are earnest in our request, if we cry to God from the depths of our hearts, we can be assured that such prayer must have its origin in God and therefore be acceptable to him."[35]

Notice the words *earnest, depths,* and *assured.* "Earnestness in prayer is a sign God hears our prayers, as fire kindled from heaven sheweth God accepts the sacrifice."[36] Prayer that is earnest is prayer that is answerable.

The Attitude of Intensity

Akin to the attitude of earnestness is the attitude of intensity. They are not the same, but they are interactive with each other. If we pray without one, we will likely pray without the other.

Earnestness relates to the heart—the inner attitude of the praying Christian. Intensity relates to the outward practice of prayer. When we do something with intensity, we do it with every fiber of our being. I always am intrigued as I stand at the Western Wall in Jerusalem and watch the Hasidic Jews bobbing and weaving as they pray. They go through this erratic motion with such intensity of body. Unfortunately, many of them are modern-day Pharisees—all show and no glow.

When we come to the Lord with a pressing need, our prayers should reflect the intensity of that need. In a very real sense, our prayers should demonstrate to God our desperation. We have no hope without him. Vance Havner used to say, "The tragedy of today is that the situation is desperate but the saints are not." God must sometimes feel that way about us when we pray in a lackluster manner.

J. Oswald Sanders suggests why God tarries in responding to our prayers. He says, "We may be asking without greatly caring about the issue."[37] That uncaring attitude shows up in a lack of earnestness in our hearts and a lack of intensity in our prayers. It lends itself to quick prayer, infrequent prayer, and matter-of-fact prayer. It's the kind of attitude that God can say no to any time day or night. Put more of yourself into your prayer life and you will get more out of it. Pray intensely.

The Attitude of Authority

A passport is a very useful document when traveling internationally. I applied for my first passport in 1964. Since that time I have gone through five passports. All have expired, been destroyed, or received too many stamps to continue using. I have had additional pages added to existing passports to permit their continued use. My passport always looks like the one you see in those travel guides.

A passport isn't very attractive (especially the photo). It isn't very large. It isn't very thick. It isn't particularly interesting to read. So what makes it so valuable? Authority. It gives me the authority to go just about anywhere in the world. Behind this document stands the full authority of the United States government. I travel to other countries only in the authority of my passport.

Authority is a wonderful thing. Occasionally one of my staff will make a request of another and add, "This is what Dr. Kroll wants." That little added note strengthens the authority of the request. That's what authority is—a convincing power to influence.

When we come to God in prayer, we must come with authority. The people of Jesus' day were amazed at the authority with which he taught (Mark 1:22, 27). God wants us to come to him in that same authority. The Savior said, "You may ask me for anything in my name, and I will do it" (John 14:14). This authority is in his person, not in our asking. Saul of Tarsus, before his conversion, went to Damascus "with the authority and commission of the chief priests" (Acts 26:12). But after his conversion, Paul the apostle went to the throne of God with even greater authority and commission.

When you pray, come humbly, but do not approach God with the attitude that you have no right. You have every right because you have Jesus as Savior and Lord. When you present your passport to the passport control agent of another country, you do so with authority—your country's authority. When you go to God in prayer, you do so with authority—your Savior's authority. If you don't go with this attitude, you may go away without his stamp in your passport.

The Attitude of Confidence

Just as the attitudes of earnestness and intensity are interrelated, so too are the attitudes of authority and confidence. Authority is external; confidence is internal. Authority is fixed; confidence fluctuates. Authority is the basis for our actions; confidence is acting on that basis. Prayer needs both.

Our prayer attitude is improper if we come to God lacking confidence. Remember, "without faith it is impossible to please God, because anyone who comes to him must believe that he exists and that he rewards those who earnestly seek him" (Heb. 11:6). If we lack confidence in God's existence, if we lack confidence in his ability to answer, or if we lack confidence that he will hear us, we come to God with an attitude that begs him to deny our petitions.

Read what John says in his first epistle. "This is the confidence that we have in approaching God: that if we ask anything according to his will, he hears us" (1 John 5:14). There is no point in praying to God if we do not have confidence in him. Donald G. Bloesch suggests, "To be unfailing effective, prayer must be offered in the assurance of faith, for to doubt the ability or mercy of God is to sin against him. We should doubt ourselves, our own piety, our own worthiness, but we should never doubt the promises of God given in Holy Scripture."[38] To this Lehman Strauss adds, "Faith takes the promises of God, and says, 'I am confident that it will be exactly as God said it will be, because I have confidence in God.'"[39]

To pray with a lack of confidence says to God, "I don't trust you." That's a deniable attitude that leads to deniable prayer.

The Attitude of Boldness

If we have confidence in God, that confidence will give rise to a holy boldness when we pray that otherwise would be unknown to us. Confidence in the promises of God gives us boldness in prayer. Read of the boldness of Abraham (Gen. 18:23–32) or the boldness of Moses (Exod. 33:12–18). These men asked for things that most of us would only dream of being bold enough to ask for. Still, their attitudes were right before God.

Today we have spawned a generation of people who are bold in prayer. They have boldness to ask for anything, anytime, anywhere. They simply tell God what they want and lay claim to it. Name it and claim it. These people may have a problem with humility but certainly not with boldness. We must remember, however, that before Abraham prayed boldly in Genesis 18, he walked obediently in chapter 12, gave unselfishly in chapter 13, acted bravely in chapter 14, trusted implicitly in chapter 15, and walked blamelessly in chapter 17.

Approaching God boldly is not the same as approaching him brashly. Abraham was not perfect; he acted brashly on occasion, as we all do. But when he prayed, he did not pray brashly. He prayed confidently and without timidity because of his relationship with God. We must do the same if we do not want God to deny our prayers.

Remember, "We do not have a high priest who is unable to sympathize with our weaknesses, but we have one who has been tempted in every way, just as we are—yet was without sin. Let us then approach the throne of grace with confidence" (Heb. 4:15–16). God blesses the boldness of faith in him but not the brashness of presuming upon him. Come to God boldly. If you don't come boldly, why come at all?

The Attitude of Helplessness

This attitude gets prayers answered. When we come to God with the idea that he is one of many options, we go away looking for another option. If we pray trusting in the slightest glimmer of hope in someone or something else, we cannot possibly express complete and exclusive trust in God. In short, until we are helpless, we often remain prayerless, and that's not good.

There's a very touching account in 1 Samuel 22 about the attitude of helplessness. David was on the run from King Saul. When he left Gath and came to the cave of Adullam, four hundred of his kinsmen from Judah allied themselves with him and quickly became his ragtag army. "All those who were in distress or in debt or discontented gathered around him, and he became their leader" (1 Sam. 22:2).

These men were not a fierce fighting force. In fact, most of them were desperate misfits. Their strength was in their helplessness and David's help. They came to him offering nothing but loyalty. They were like you and me before God—

desperate misfits, not a fierce fighting force. Yet when we approach God with an attitude of helplessness, we find his help at our disposal.

God is not looking for your strength when you pray. What strength do you have anyway? He is pleased when you come to him in your helplessness, for when you are weak, then he makes you strong. When your strength is drained, when your finances are depleted, when your hope is almost gone, pray. Come to God in your helplessness and weakness and receive his help and strength. That's an attitude he won't deny when you pray.

The Attitude of Emptiness

Can one attitude be more important than others in getting answers to our prayers? Maybe not. But when we talk about what will keep God from answering our prayers, there can be no more detrimental attitude than being full of ourselves. If we pray without the attitude of emptiness, we pray a divinely deniable prayer.

In Africa, Asia, South America, Europe, the Middle East, Australia, North America, and elsewhere I have known some of God's choicest saints. What made them so choice was not their silver tongue that enabled them to move large audiences nor their keen intellect that allowed them to reason circles around others. What made them choice was their brokenness before God. On my knees I have heard them weep for their unsaved families. I have heard saints whose hearts were broken pray that God would forgive their sins. I have brushed away tears as I heard them ask God to burden their souls for their church. Their emptiness of self and fullness of the Spirit was an embarrassment to me. They had found the secret of praying undeniable prayers. They touched the heart of God.

The following poem appropriately expresses the attitude of emptiness.

> One by one He took them from me,
> All the things I valued most.
> Until I was empty-handed,
> Every glittering toy was lost.
> And I walked earth's highways grieving,
> In my ranks of poverty,
> Until I heard his voice inviting,
> "Lift those empty hands to me."
> Then I turned my hands toward heaven,
> And He filled them with a store,
> Of all His own transcendent riches,
> Until they could contain no more.
> At last I comprehended,
> With my stupid mind and dull,
> That God cannot pour out His riches,
> Into hands already full.[40]

When you pray, do you come to God with your hands full and your heart empty? Or do you come with a full heart and empty hands? Your attitude in prayer often determines how answerable your prayers are. Come to God in brokenness. Come in tears. Come empty-handed. Let him fill you with the goodness that only heaven can provide.

What's a Person to Do?

Our attitudes often determine God's answers. If you are wondering why God isn't answering your prayers, check your attitudes. Attitude deficiency can bankrupt you more quickly than asset inadequacy. After all, God is the one who supplies all your needs. If you approach him with attitudes that make your prayers deniable, you have cut the supply line to your own happiness, abundance, peace, and joy.

Victor Frankl, the eminent German Jewish doctor, was arrested by the Gestapo during World War II. As he was being interrogated by the Nazi secret police, Frankl was stripped of all his possessions—his clothes, his jewelry, even his wedding band. His head was shaved. He was repeatedly taken from his prison cell, placed under bright lights, and questioned for hours. He underwent many savage, senseless tortures. But Frankl realized there was one thing the Nazi goons couldn't take from him. He thought, "I still have the power to choose my own attitudes."

You have the power to choose your own attitudes too, even when it comes to prayer. Regardless of what others believe or do, you can choose what attitudes you will bring with you when you pray. If you believe prayer will work, if you think God will hear, if you are convinced you have removed the prayer blockers in your life, you can pray with confidence. If you believe prayer is a gimmick, a ritual, or a childish wish, your attitude may well deter God's answer. Attitude is vital in being empowered in prayer.

Make some serious attitude adjustments before you next pray, and then watch out. God is more anxious to answer than you are to pray. When attitudes that cause him to deny your prayers are adjusted, the answers just keep on coming like the hits on a Top 40 station.

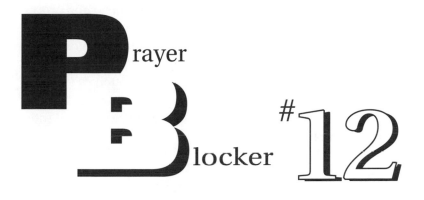

Prayer Blocker #12

God doesn't answer when

We Quit Too Soon

My center is giving way, my right is retreating. Situation excellent. I shall attack.

Field Marshall Ferdinand Foch

Prayer is the supreme act of hope. If we pray, we must believe someone is there to hear our prayer and is powerful enough to answer us. Prayer that is permeated with hope hears the inaudible, believes the inconceivable, and expresses the inexpressible. It lifts us from the ditch of despair and transports us to the throne room of God. But prayer without hope is like a sail without wind. It's going nowhere.

Hope and prayer are very compatible comrades. They are an unbeatable tag team. Each alone is powerful, but together they are dynamite. They complement each other wonderfully. Like a pair of hands, hope reaches out to God in the dark while prayer folds in silent submission to whatever God's answer will be. What one does not accomplish alone, they accomplish in tandem.

The product of this partnership between hope and prayer is perseverance. That's prayer that keeps on praying and won't quit. Like the Energizer bunny, it keeps on going and going and going. I suspect that often, when God doesn't answer our prayers, it's because we quit too soon. We lacked hope, and without it there can be no persistence. Unlike the famous pink bunny, we keep on going and going, and then one day we just quit.

In Praise of Dogged Determination

While there are great and admirable people who seem to burst quickly onto the scene like the latest country singer, most men and women who make a perceptible contribution to time or eternity take the long road to notoriety. Their success is not overnight but rather over time. They are the plodders, the people who labor in obscurity for years until one day the world "discovers" them. I appreciate this kind of dogged determination.

The Nurse

Born in Florence, Italy, in the home of a wealthy English gentleman, most of her childhood was spent on the posh family estate in Derbyshire, England. At age seventeen her heart was touched by hurting people, and she became consumed with the desire to relieve suffering. She was appalled by the unsanitary conditions in hospitals. Convinced that God was calling her to be a nurse, she enrolled in the Institute of St. Vincent de Paul in Paris. Consequently, she both ministered to the hurting and changed forever the standards under which hospitals operated.

The road that is God's will is never without potholes, as Florence Nightingale soon learned. She had to overcome the opposition of a neurotic mother and sister, the Victorian taboo against women pursuing a career, the jealous antagonism of the male-dominated medical profession, and the objections of army brass. But Florence believed in prayer. She persistently prayed that God would open doors for her, and he did. When the Crimean War broke out, Florence volunteered as a nurse and turned a vermin-infested, overcrowded hospital in Turkey, which had a death rate of 42 percent, into a sanitary house of mercy, with a death rate of only 2 percent.

Florence Nightingale believed God wanted her to be a nurse. She became the most famous nurse in history, but only after she prayed with stubborn persistence that God would open doors for her. When it comes to prayer, don't quit too soon.

The President

Abraham Lincoln was perhaps America's most beloved president. He would have been the first to admit that he wasn't perfect, but he was a man of decency and morality. He received much of his character training at his mother's knee. Lincoln said, "All that I am or hope to be, I owe to my angel mother." Abraham Lincoln's mother was a woman of prayer, and she taught her son never to quit praying.

Lincoln's rise in American politics was not without its setbacks. Still, no setback was equal to the persistent prayers of the sixteenth president.

In 1832, Lincoln was a candidate for the Illinois state legislature. He lost. He ran again in 1834 and this time won. In 1846 he was elected to the U.S. House of Representatives but only served one term. He wasn't even renominated by his own party. He campaigned for Zachary Taylor for president, hoping to be appointed Commissioner of the General Land Office. He wasn't. In 1854 he again ran for the legislature and won, but resigned hoping the new Anti-Nebraska party would support him for the Senate. They didn't.

Dogged determination and a sense of God's hand on his life kept Abraham Lincoln on his knees in prayer. He was nominated as vice president of the United States in 1856, but his party lost. In 1858 he ran again for the U.S. Senate, and again he lost. Then, after years of patience and persistent prayer, in 1860 he was simply nominated as a "favorite son" from Illinois, and Abraham Lincoln was elected the sixteenth president of the United States. When it comes to prayer, don't quit too soon.

The Neighbor

Unlike Florence Nightingale or Abraham Lincoln, you probably won't recognize his name. It's John Williams. Everybody just called him "Old John." He never ran for public office; he probably wouldn't have been elected anyway. His family was not wealthy, and he did not enjoy the privilege of travel. His contributions to time and eternity were not in the realm of government or medicine. But his prayers were just as persistent and just as effective as those of the nurse or the president.

Old John was a godly man. For him a handshake was as binding as a written contract. He was in church every Sunday and on his knees during the early hours of each day. Old John was a man of persistent prayer.

One day an evangelistic meeting was held in his small town, and a very old man—even older than Old John—stepped out from his pew and came forward. He was gloriously saved, and while the congregation looked on in silence, Old John joined the man. With tears in his eyes, Old John told how fifty years ago twenty-five young people of that church made a pledge to pray every day for this man's salvation. Said Old John, "I am the only one still living to see the prayers of fifty years answered." For this good neighbor, fifty years was not too long to persevere in prayer. When it comes to prayer, don't quit too soon.

The Wrestler

Persistent plodders should be praised. Edward Gibbon spent twenty-six years writing *The History of the Decline and Fall of the Roman Empire*. Noah Webster worked diligently for thirty-six years on the first edition of his dictionary. The Roman orator Cicero practiced before friends every day for thirty years in order to perfect his public speaking. The only person for whom persistence does not pay is the person who quits too soon.

That's as true in prayer as in anything else. The inspiring story of Jacob's all-night wrestling match with God's angel demonstrates the benefits of persisting in prayer. When the angel saw that he could not overpower Jacob, he touched the socket of Jacob's hip, crippling him and said, "Let me go, for it is daybreak." Jacob persisted, "I will not let you go unless you bless me" (Gen. 32:26).

Is it possible that God didn't answer your prayers because you quit too soon? You wrestle with God throughout the night until 6:00 A.M. and quit, when the answer would have come at 6:15 A.M. had you only persisted. None of us will ever know how much prayer became ineffective for the lack of just a little more. Dogged determination in praying for your family, your church, your unsaved neighbor, or your prodigal son or daughter is frequently the key that unlocks the heart of God. When it comes to prayer, don't quit too soon.

The Importance of Importunity

It's a word we don't often use anymore—*importunity*. But it's a good word. *Importunity* means to urge a request on someone with persistence. It's used in the King James Version in the parable of Luke 11:8. Actually, the word is more akin to our English word *shameless*. When you pray with importunity, you persistently and shamelessly request something of God. *Importunity* is just an old word for an old concept—don't quit too soon.

Importunity is important, especially in prayer. Unless God has refused our request, he never tires of our asking him. The former Archbishop of Canterbury, William Temple (1881–1944), said it this way: "God does not grant petitions in order to rid Himself of the nuisance which we become by our persistence. . . . Scarcely anything deepens and purifies faith in God . . . as surely as perseverance in prayer."[41]

God doesn't tire of our shameless persistence in prayer. In fact, he encourages it. Don't confuse importunity with imposition. Never say, "Oh, I don't want to bother God with that again. It's just an imposition." An imposition is an unwanted and unwarranted forcing of yourself on someone else, but when you come to God you're not forcing yourself on him. He has invited you to come. "Ask and it will be given to you; seek and you will find; knock and the door will be opened to you" (Luke 11:9). Sincere persistence in prayer is never an imposition to God. Don't think that it is.

Jesus spoke two great parables to teach us that shameless persistence in prayer is the right thing to do. Both parables are recorded by Luke. Let's see what we can learn from each about not quitting too soon when we pray.

Open All Night

With the advent of 7-Eleven, Circle K, and other convenience stores, the words "open all night" have taken on clearer meaning. There is never a time—day or night—when you cannot buy a loaf of bread, a can of Coke, or a pack of gum. But while we think of "open all night" in reference to a twenty-four-hour diner or a convenience store, Jesus used this concept to teach us something about shameless persistence in prayer. His parable is recorded in Luke 11:5–8.

Picture this. It's late. You're just about to turn in when there's a knock at the door. It's a friend you haven't seen in months. He's on his way to a business meeting in another state but is too tired to drive any further. He wants to know if he can spend the night with you. Sure he can. "Come right in," you say. "Have you eaten? I'll whip up a little something for you." Then you discover you're out of milk, bread, and bologna—the staples of life. The convenience store is several miles away, so you decide just to pop across the street and ask your neighbor for the things you need.

When you knock on the neighbor's door you hear a voice inside say, "Go away! We're trying to sleep in here." Obviously he doesn't recognize your knock so you say, "Bill, it's me—your neighbor. I just need to borrow some bread and a few other things." Bill is unimpressed. "Stop banging on that door. Do you want to wake my kids?"

Jesus' parable doesn't sound dated at all, does it? In fact, it's timeless. The point is clear. While you would expect the neighbor to accommodate your midnight need simply because he is a hospitable neighbor, nevertheless it is your persistence that rouses him to action. Bill was not about to open the door, but shameless persistence did the trick.

Jesus contrasts the neighbor's reluctance and selfishness with the openness and generosity of our heavenly Father. His argument runs like this: If the self-centered neighbor, who cherished his sleep more than his neighbor, reluctantly rose at midnight to supply a need, how much more will God's heart be moved by your persistent prayers to supply your need. If persistence was the key to an unwilling heart, how much more effective will persistence be to the willing heart of God.

Don't get caught thinking it's too late to go to God. It's never too late. He's open all night. Keep praying. Your persistent knocking on heaven's door anytime day or night shows God that you mean business. You're sincere, unlike the little boy whom the preacher saw standing on his tiptoes to reach the doorbell on the neighbor's front porch. The preacher approached, picked up the boy, and helped him ring the bell. Then the man asked, "Now what do we do?" The little rascal replied, "Now we run like crazy so we don't get caught."

God wants you to ring heaven's bell again and again. But he doesn't want you to ring and run away. Prayer is not a lark; it's your lifeline to God. Get serious about prayer. God may not answer the first time, but don't let that discourage you. Don't quit too soon. Persistence pays. It brought a bologna sandwich and a glass of milk to a weary traveler. It will bring you what you need from God.

Jesus' own application of this parable is instructive. "So I say to you: Ask and it will be given to you; seek and you will find; knock and the door will be opened to you" (Luke 11:9). That's quite a promise. In fact, it's a threefold exhortation followed by a threefold promise.

When we pray we are either consciously or unconsciously admitting that we have a need and only God can meet that need. The verb is one used when an inferior makes a request of a superior. We ask because we know we are impotent. We ask God because we know he is omnipotent.

While asking implies humility, seeking implies action. We do more than ask; we actively seek an answer to our prayer. At final exams, students who ask God to bless their diligent study have an appropriate prayer. Students who ask God to bless them without any study don't have a prayer. Asking is like remembering you have no bread; seeking is leaving your house to find some.

Knocking is more than a combination of asking and seeking. It is asking and seeking with shameless persistence. Asking reminds us of our need; seeking leads us across the street to our neighbor. But the persistent knocking on his door is what successfully brings us bread.

So it is with God. Prayer has feet. Prayer seeks to find the answer and it does, but maybe not on the first knock. A literal rendering of Luke 11:9 is, "So I say to you: Keep on asking and it will be given to you; keep on seeking and you will find; keep on knocking and the door will be opened to you." Persistence is the key. If God hasn't answered your prayers yet, keep at it. You may be just a knock and a prayer away. Don't quit too soon.

The Rogue Judge

Jesus' second parable designed to teach us that we "should always pray and not give up" (Luke 18:1) is about an unprincipled, unjust, uncaring judge (Luke 18:2–5). He was appointed to a high office, but he didn't have the character to belong there. He never asked himself, "How would God have me to rule in this case?" or even, "What is best for the defendant in this case?" This judge simply did what he wanted. He had no respect for the rule of law nor any sympathy for the oppressed people who appeared before him. He was a rogue judge without love for justice or mankind.

Here's the scenario. A widow appeared before this unjust judge, not once but many times. Day after day she came to the judge's courtroom to plead for justice. Day after day the rude judge rebuffed her. Apparently the woman had been denied some benefit to which she was entitled. All she wanted was what was right. All the judge wanted was to be rid of her. She went home disappointed day after day.

The woman knew her cause was right, so she persisted. In fact, she shamelessly persisted. She had learned the art of importunity. Finally the judge, ready to pull out his hair, said, "I will see that she gets justice, so that she won't eventually wear me out with her coming!" (Luke 18:5). Persistence had won the day; so had justice.

Truth by Contrast

It is evident that in neither of Jesus' parables is there correspondence between the characters and God. After all, these are parables—plausible stories designed to teach ethical truth. God is not the reluctantly helpful neighbor in the first parable, nor is he the unjust judge in the second parable. Jesus was using contrast to teach truth—a comparison between unholy men and a holy God.

J. Oswald Sanders comments, "In both parables, Jesus is careful to vindicate the character of God and to reveal His true nature and attitude. . . . God is neither a selfish neighbor nor a crooked judge. . . . The lesson is that lukewarmness in prayer, as in everything else, is nauseating to God, and comes away empty-handed. On the other hand, shameless persistence, the importunity that will not be denied, returns with the answer in its hands."[42]

If an unworthy, sinful, self-seeking judge will finally act because of a woman's persistence, how much more willingly your loving, kind, and compassionate heavenly Father will act as a result of your persistent prayers. Keep on praying. Your potential for success is enormous. Don't quit too soon.

Good Company

If we are persistent in praying, we're in very good company. If we quit too soon, I'd hesitate to brag about my companions.

The early church stubbornly prayed for Peter when he was in prison (Acts 12:5). In fact, when he was miraculously released and came to the house of Mary where the disciples had gathered, they were still praying for him (v. 12). That's persistent praying. That's the kind of company we want to be in.

After defeating the prophets of Baal on Mount Carmel, Elijah prayed for the return of rain (1 Kings 18:16–43). He sent his servant to look for any sign of rain. Nothing. He prayed again. Still nothing. Seven times he prayed, and seven times he sent his servant to look for rain. Finally, on the seventh time, there appeared "a cloud as small as a man's hand

... rising from the sea" (1 Kings 18:44). That's persistent praying. That's the kind of company we want to be in.

The church has prayed for nearly two thousand years, "Even so, come, Lord Jesus" (Rev. 22:20 KJV). He hasn't come yet. Should we quit? Not a chance. Not if we want to be in good company—the company of the persistent. God has his own reasons for delaying his responses to your prayers. Do not weary of doing well. Keep on praying. "Be still before the LORD and wait patiently for him" (Ps. 37:7). Answers to your prayers will come if you don't quit too soon.

How Long Should We Pray?

Asking how long we should pray is not a bad question for a chapter on quitting too soon. Is it always too soon to quit? How do we know when we should stop praying for something? Every serious man or woman of prayer has wondered about this.

I wish I could give you a clever answer, but something like, "pray until you can't pray anymore" won't help you much. Some of you already feel a bit "prayed out." Are there some guidelines in God's Word about how long we should pray? Yes there are. Let's think about some of them.

Pray Until the Impossible Becomes Improbable

When something is impossible that means it cannot happen; when it is improbable that means it is not likely to happen. You may say, "My Johnny will never make the dean's list; it's impossible." Of course without knowing Johnny I can't say for sure, but it's more likely you mean that it's improbable he will make the dean's list. One day he may achieve this honor, but with his current 1.35 GPA, it's very improbable.

Should we pray for the impossible? Why not? God is the God of the impossible. Don't limit him. "With God all things are possible" (Matt. 19:26). But while God can do the impossible, he is not likely to do the improbable. He has the capability, but he is not likely to use it.

For example, you invite a fine young preacher to candidate for the pastoral position at your church. He is a very skillful homiletician, a gifted communicator. His personality is warm and friendly. He's perfect for your church, or any other church for that matter. You pray that he will accept your church's call to be pastor. It seems impossible, but you persistently pray for the impossible. That's commendable. Praying for the impossible is simply praying with great faith.

But if this fine young preacher accepts the call to another pastorate, is it probable he will also accept your call? It is possible he could pastor both churches, but is not likely. So what should you do? If he informs you that he has accepted another call, stop praying that he will become your pastor and move on. When the impossible becomes improbable, it's time to refocus your prayers. That's how to know when you've prayed long enough.

Pray Until God Gives an Answer

God both opens doors and closes them. Pray for either, but when God gives an answer that doesn't match your prayers, it's time to change your prayers.

During the decade of the '80s, I was a college president. I enjoyed immensely what I was doing. Often I would receive invitations to assume the leadership at other colleges, but each time I said no without a moment's hesitation. I was where God wanted me, and I knew it. But in January 1990, God convinced me to be open to something else. What else, I didn't know. In February 1990, Back to the Bible invited me to consider becoming their Bible teacher. I prayed, "God, give me direction." I looked for clues, but they were hard to come by. I looked for help, but few could provide it. All I could do was pray.

Back to the Bible's board had unanimously invited me to join them in Lincoln, Nebraska, but I needed an answer from God. I prayed more earnestly, persistently, stubbornly, importunately. Should my answer be yes or no? I didn't know.

Finally, when meeting with the board, I said to them, "I have read the job description. What I want to know is, what do you really want me to do?" One godly man said, "We want you to spend enough time with God each day so that when you come to the microphone you have something to say." There was my answer. God had put those words in that man's mouth to speak to me. When God's answer came, my prayers for guidance stopped.

Pray until you are sure God has answered you, and when he has, move on in your prayer focus. You've prayed about that need long enough.

Pray Until You Know the Answer Is on the Way

Sometimes when you pray God gives you an inward, quiet assurance that he is going to answer you in a certain way. When he assures you, it's not necessary to continue praying for that request. God's assurance is as good as his performance. Just make sure it's God's assurance and not your own wishful desire.

Perhaps God has given you the gift of faith (1 Cor. 12:7–9) and you have a supernatural ability to believe the answer is on the way (see chap. 5). Perhaps it's not a spiritual gift as much as it is an internal peace from God. You just know God will answer, and you know what God's answer will be. Most of us have had this experience at some time.

The prophet Micah said, "I wait for God my Savior; my God will hear me" (Micah 7:7). When you "approach God with freedom and confidence" (Eph. 3:12), you can "lie down and sleep" (Ps. 3:5) knowing that additional prayer will not alter the outcome. "This is the confidence we have in approaching God: that if we ask anything according to his will, he hears us. And if we know that he hears us—whatever we ask—we know that we have what we asked of him" (1 John 5:14–15). That confidence means you can stop praying when you know the answer is on its way. You have prayed long enough.

Pray Until God Says No

We also can stop praying when God says no. How will we know when he says no? Sometimes God says no through his Word. We have prayed for something, and in the normal course of reading our Bible we discover that what we prayed for can never be God's will. We have God's answer; the answer is no.

At other times we know God has said no because our circumstances change. Your young family has been growing, and you need more room in your house. You have prayed that God would give you a new house with adequate space. But instead of buying a new house further out in the suburbs, your neighbors volunteer to help you add a couple of rooms to your existing house. It will save you a ton of money. Your circumstances have changed; you know God has said no to your request for a new house.

There are other times when the Spirit of God restrains our prayers because God has said no to our request. What we've prayed for suddenly doesn't seem right. The Spirit has taken away our desire to pray for it. We have lost interest in our request. We know the Spirit is definitely guiding us now. God has spoken through his Spirit and the answer is no. It's time to stop praying for that request and focus on another.

What's a Person to Do?

Sometimes God doesn't answer your prayers because you quit too soon. You are not as persistent, as tenacious, as steadfast as you ought to be. You feel you've prayed so often for something that God can't be interested in that request anymore, so why bother. But God is far more anxious to hear your prayers than you are to pray them.

Adoniram Judson, the great missionary to Burma, was a man of importunate prayer. He believed in praying until it was time to stop. Judson said, "God loves importunate prayer so much that he will not give us much blessing without it. And the reason he loves such prayer is that he loves us, and knows that it is a necessary preparation for our receiving the richest blessing he is waiting and longing to bestow. I never prayed sincerely and earnestly for anything but it came at some time—no matter at how distant a day, somehow, in some shape, probably the last I would have devised, it came."[43]

Persistent praying is for your benefit. It demonstrates your confidence that God will answer and prepares your heart to receive that answer. Praying with importunity allows you time to evaluate your requests and make certain they are in God's will and for his glory. If you do not pray persistently, you do not pray successfully.

So keep on praying. Just because you've prayed for someone for years and God hasn't answered yet is no indication that he is not listening to your prayers. This doesn't mean he is not interested. It simply means the answer is on the way but isn't here yet.

God wants you to bombard heaven with your prayers. He wants you to be stubbornly persistent, shamelessly tenacious in coming to him with your requests. When God doesn't answer your prayers, it could be because you have quit too soon. God delights in hearing you pray. Hang in there. Be persistent. Keep on praying. Someday God will answer. He's just that kind of God.

Prayer Unblockers

God does answer when

We Remove the Blockers

Prayer is not conquering God's reluctance, but taking hold of God's willingness.

Phillips Brooks

It was the winter of 1968. Linda and I were living in a mobile home on Topsfield Road in Ipswich, Massachusetts. I was attending seminary during the day and working at night. Linda worked as a cook at the Governor Dummer Academy during the afternoon and evening hours. Tracy and Tim, our two oldest children, were age two and a half and one and a half.

Northern Massachusetts sometimes gets heavy snow during the winter months, but nothing like the winter of 1968. Linda was at work when the snow began, and I was home with the children. The sky was full of the white stuff. I had never seen it snow like that. Soon there was a foot on the ground, then two, then more. How much snow could fall at one time? Linda phoned to say she was stranded at the academy and wouldn't be home. All roads were blocked and impassable.

Before it was all over, forty-two inches of snow had fallen. Linda and I were marooned for three days apart from each other. Ipswich was cut off from the rest of the world. On the third day, army helicopters began dropping supplies into the town. It was not until the fourth morning that huge snowplows and road graders unblocked the highways and life began to return to normal.

Whether it's the free flow of traffic or the free flow of prayer, whatever blocks our way has to be removed before things can return to normal. Our heavenly Father has paved the way for us to have a steady, vibrant, meaningful prayer life as a normal part of our Christian experience. For many Christians, however, such prayer is anything but normal. Their road to God is impeded by prayer blockers.

Obstruction Removal

Many have felt the pain of an angina attack. Angina is the direct result of insufficient blood reaching the heart muscle. Likely this is due to a blockage in one or more of the major arteries. Today a popular medical procedure for alleviating that blockage is called percutaneous transluminal coronary angioplasty (PTCA), or angioplasty for short. The doctor inserts a guide catheter into a leg or arm artery and guides it to the exact location of the blockage. Then a smaller catheter with a balloon at its tip is inserted through the guide catheter. The balloon is then inflated and deflated at the point of the obstruction to improve the blood flow to the heart.

In many respects, the Holy Spirit is the instrument God uses to perform spiritual angioplasty on us. The Spirit convicts us of cherished sin and removes the blockage. He gives us a forgiving spirit and removes the blockage. The Spirit helps us discern God's will and removes the blockage. He molds our motives and removes the blockage. The Holy Spirit helps us remove the obstacles that keep our prayers from flowing to God and his answers from flowing to us.

Once a blockage is removed, we have no guarantee that it will never return. Many people have angioplasty more than once, and some still have to resort to coronary bypass surgery. Unblocking an artery is one thing, taking steps to keep it from blocking again is quite another.

The doctor will encourage the patient to do certain things in order to reduce the risk of recurring obstructions (e.g., stress reduction, exercise, diet, and weight control). Angioplasty is a procedure designed to unblock arteries already clogged; subsequent steps are designed to keep arteries unblocked.

The same is true with prayer. Addressing the twelve prayer blockers in this book is akin to angioplasty. Keeping them from recurring will require a program of stress reduction, spiritual exercise, biblical diet, and so on. These we could call *unblockers*—those things that keep open our prayer arteries to God.

Let's explore eight specific things we can do to make our prayers more effective. These are the prayer unblockers that keep the channel open to God so that he will hear and answer our prayers.

Unblocker #1: Take the Time

How long does it take to pray in a meaningful way? Not very long. How much time do many Christians spend in prayer? Not very much. Maybe that's the problem.

We schedule appointments with the dentist. We have an appointment to get our hair cut. We plan lunch around noon. We watch the evening news on television at exactly the same time each night. We pray . . .

In the Muslim religion, followers of Islam stop five times a day, kneel face down in straight rows, and pray to Allah at the call to prayer. Most do it faithfully, time after time, day after day. It doesn't matter where they are; they stop to pray. But we Christians pride ourselves on not being so mechanical, so legalistic. We can pray anytime we want. We don't have to have a predetermined time. And because we have no set time, we do not take the time either.

Pray anytime you need to talk with God, but plan a specific time each day in which you have a meaningful time of prayer. I prefer early in the morning before my day has had a chance to fall apart. I want God to get me when I'm fresh. Besides, there is a principle running through the pages of Scripture. It's the principle of the firstfruits. God is to have the first of our fields, the first of our flocks, the first of our family, the first of our funds. To be consistent, I believe he deserves the first of our day as well. Plan a special time each day when you can be alone with God.

Whatever you do, don't hurry away from your time with God. Scottish clergyman Alexander Whyte said, "Much mischief to our souls . . . lies in the way that we stint, and starve, and scamp our prayers by hurrying over them. Prayer worth calling prayer, prayer that God will call true prayer and will treat as true prayer, takes far more time by the clock than one man in a thousand thinks."[44] Prayer that God finds worthy of answer is prayer that is unhurried, offered by those who take the time to commune with God.

"But I can't take the time," you object. Can't take the time for God? Can't take the time to spend a few minutes with the only one who can answer your prayers? If you think you can't take the time, do what I did. Buy an alarm clock. I find the time to eat. I find the time to sleep. I find the time to read the newspaper. How must God feel when I cannot find the time to pray?

Meaningful conversation with God is essential to unblock the prayer blockers. It's also essential to keep your prayer arteries unblocked. Tomorrow, make an appointment with God and keep it.

Unblocker #2: Pick the Place

Bible personalities prayed in some pretty unusual places. Paul prayed in the temple (Acts 21:26; 22:17), and he prayed in prison (Acts 16:25). As a dynamic preacher, Paul prayed on the Mediterranean seashore (Acts 21:5). As a disobedient prophet, Jonah prayed in the belly of a fish in the Mediterranean (Jonah 2). Elijah prayed in victory on the top of Mount Carmel (1 Kings 18:42); he prayed in defeat under a scrubby tree in the wilderness (1 Kings 19:4). We can pray anywhere. Jesus also prayed in diverse places:

He prayed in the flowing waters of the Jordan (Luke 3:21).

He prayed in the barrenness of the wilderness (Luke 5:16).

He prayed with his disciples in the upper room (John 17).

He prayed alone in the Garden of Gethsemane (Matt. 26:36).

When Jesus had opportunity to choose a place to pray, do you remember where he most often prayed? He headed for the hills:

After feeding the five thousand, Jesus picked a hill rising from the Sea of Galilee on which to pray (Matt. 14:23).

He prayed at Caesarea Philippi in the foothills of Mount Hermon (Matt. 16:13; Luke 9:18).

He prayed on the Mount of Transfiguration (Luke 9:28).

We should also choose a place for prayer. For me, the place of choice is my study. When that alarm clock pierces the tranquility of my sleep, I get up immediately and go downstairs to my study. There I do three things in my quiet time with God. First, I read his Word for enjoyment and inspiration. Then I worship, praise, and petition him in prayer. And finally, I sit quietly and wait, just in case he wants to impress something on me. For you, the place of prayer may be an easy chair, the kitchen table, out on the deck, in the family room, or wherever. One place is as good as another, with the possible exception of the bedroom.

Generations of godly parents have taught their children to say their prayers before going to bed. This may be a good way to cap off their day, but the bed is not the place to do serious prayer. C. S. Lewis said, "No one in his senses, if he has any power of ordering his own day, would reserve his chief prayers for bedtime—obviously the worst possible hour for any action which needs concentration."[45]

Lewis is right. Pick a place to pray, but for adults, at night in bed probably isn't it. God deserves more of our attention. Pick the right place to pray, and let the unblockers keep the arteries open to God.

Unblocker #3: Ban Interruptions

Jack was a successful businessman. Although he owned the company, he was appreciated by his employees as a team player. He had an open-door policy; anybody could discuss anything with him at any time. Well, almost any time. It was an invariable rule that no one entered his office from nine to ten each morning. Everybody knew it; everybody respected it. Jack set aside that time strictly for private prayer. No interruptions. No exceptions.

Men and women in his command loved General Lovelace. He was tough but fair. He was 100 percent army. Things were done by the book or they were not done at all. Still, soldiers never bothered him when they saw a white handkerchief tied to the front of his tent. The general was in prayer. No interruptions. No exceptions.

E. M. Bounds has written much on the subject of prayer. With regard to spending time alone with God, no interruptions allowed, Bounds said, "God's acquaintance is not made hurriedly. He does not bestow His gifts on the casual or hasty comer and goer. To be much alone with God is the secret of knowing Him and of influence with Him."[46]

Interruptions are a part of life. The phone rings, you run to answer it. The doorbell chimes, you hurry to see who's there. The alarm goes off on your computer, you're late for a meeting. You are a busy person. But activity is no substitute for spirituality, even if our activity is ministry. Each of us needs a time out with God—perhaps fifteen minutes or a half hour a day—in which it's just God and you.

I need a few uninterrupted minutes when no one wants me to jelly their bread, sign their off-duty form, or answer their questions. I need uninterrupted time with God, and so do you. Each day, "take time to be holy." Make it uninterrupted time. Don't answer the phone, don't invite others into the room, don't let your mind wander to other things. That's God's time. Make it the most enjoyable time of your day.

Unblocker #4: Be Positive

To make your prayers more effective, make them more positive. Positive prayer is solution-centered, not problem-centered. It keeps the passageway to God unblocked.

A study on attitudes in prayer at the University of Redlands found that those who focused on negative things in prayer usually failed to see answers to their prayers. Is anybody surprised? Negative prayer produces negative results. If God were a negative God, we would expect negative prayer to be to his liking. But God is a positive God. Even the Ten Commandments, which are couched in negative language, are designed to give us a positive experience in life. It's little wonder that our prayers seem to go unheard and unanswered by God. He is looking for something positive, and we keep giving him something negative.

Maybe we can turn negative prayers into positive ones just by rephrasing them. Instead of praying, "Lord, this pain in my hip is killing me. If you don't take it away soon I'll just die," try this: "Lord, you have some good reason for this pain in my hip. Help me to gain some insight today into how I can use it to glorify you." Sound too spiritual? All right, try this. Instead of praying, "Lord, you know how that new girl in accounting brings out the worst in me. Help me to control my lust when I see her," pray something like this: "Lord, direct my day so that my eyes do not meet up with that new girl in accounting. And if they do, direct my mind to thoughts that please you."

We all have to pray about problems, but we should focus our prayers on God's solutions rather than on how nasty our problems are. Instead of worrying about doubt, pray for faith. Instead of whining about need, pray for supply. Negativity is a prayer blocker. Pray positively and you'll pray more effectively.

Unblocker #5: Target Your Prayer

One of the current buzzwords in the business community is *market segmentation*. During the last decade businesses around the world discovered that the only safe haven for business is finding a niche and being the best in that niche. As a result, companies have been downsizing and targeting their market.

A perfect example of this is the publishing industry. Years ago we used to read *Life* magazine. There was also *Look* magazine and, of course, *National Geographic*. Each of these was or continues to be a general publication, designed for everyone—moms and dads, grandparents and kids, male and female. But things are changing.

Now we have a spate of magazines just for men or just for women. In fact, some of them are just for single women or just for African-American men or just for southern grandparents. The target audience has become very specific. Sports magazines have always been popular. Now you can buy sports magazines dedicated just to football, just to baseball, just to golf—amateur golf, amateur golf for left-handed putters, ad infinitum, ad nauseam.

Maybe the business world is on to something here. Maybe we don't receive answers to our prayers because our prayers are not target specific. Maybe we should lift up one or two people to the Lord each time we pray rather than a dozen.

When I first began to teach the Bible on radio, I was overwhelmed by the responsibility. More than ten million people would hear me each day, just in North America. How could I speak to ten million? The number was just too enormous. I couldn't do it. But then I learned that I wasn't actually speaking to ten million. I was only speaking to you. Each of those ten million people was just one person. When I began to talk just with you, I began to communicate meaningfully to ten million others.

Prayer is like that. We can't pray for every country in the world, for every mission agency, or for every lost sinner every time we pray. The task is too great. Don't try. Instead, pray for one country per day. Get a copy of Patrick Johnstone's helpful book *Operation World* (Zondervan) and focus on a few missionaries in Afghanistan today, a few more some place else tomorrow, and eventually your prayers will take you all the way to the missionaries in Zimbabwe.

Use the principle of market segmentation when you pray. When you shoot shotgun prayers at problems, all you get are fragmented problems. Take aim; target your prayers. It will keep the blockages from forming.

Unblocker #6: Set Intermediate Goals

Charlie Brown was on the mound. "Strike three," the umpire yelled. Charlie groaned. "I'll never make it to the major leagues," he said. "I just don't have what it takes." Lucy approached the mound to offer her sage advice. "What you need, Charlie Brown, are some intermediate goals. Try walking off the mound without falling down."

Does it seem like your prayers are hitting a brick wall? Maybe you can unblock your prayers simply by focusing on tomorrow's solutions rather than those a year from now. We all tend to pray through a telescope.

Your neighbor Sam is not a Christian. You pray consistently for his salvation, but nothing seems to be happening. Maybe you should focus on some intermediate goals rather than the final goal of eternal salvation. For example, pray that you'll be a good neighbor to Sam. Pray you'll earn his respect and trust. Ask God to bring something into your life that the two of you have in common. Pray that his family will accept your invitation to a backyard barbecue next week. Pray that Sam will develop a thirsty curiosity in the Bible and that he will come to you for answers to his questions. These are intermediate goals that may well lead to your ultimate goal—Sam's eternal salvation.

If it seems that your prayers are still being blocked, unblock them. Ask God to open a few windows before he opens a door. Break your ultimate prayer goals down into some intermediate ones and go for some small successes. When you do, you may be surprised at how many prayers God answers right away.

Unblocker #7: Focus on the Savior

If I have learned anything about success in prayer, it is to focus on the Savior. So often when God's people pray, they fail to consciously enjoy the presence of Jesus in their prayers. This is true in other areas of life as well.

William Russell Maltby, a great Methodist preacher, gave this advice to young preachers: "You preach the Gospel;

therefore, no demand without the gift; no diagnosis without the cure. One word about sin; ten for the Saviour."[47] Alexander Whyte used to go for long walks on Saturday mornings with his friend Marcus Dods. Once Whyte commented, "Whatever we started off with in our conversation, we soon made across country, somehow, to Jesus of Nazareth." That's focusing on the Savior.

Successful prayer is more than a ploy to get what you want from God. It's a time to enjoy his presence. I find that I enjoy my minutes and hours with God much more if I spend some of them in musing about his Son—his love, his life, his compassion, his death, his resurrection, his promises. We all know that prayer should be a time of praise as well as a time of petition, but many of us have difficulty articulating that praise. When a sinner saved by Jesus' sacrifice at Calvary focuses on the Savior, thinking of things to be thankful for is never a problem.

After renowned missionary Jonathan Goforth had spoken in a chapel in southern China, a man asked to talk with him. He said, "I have heard you speak three times, and you always have the same theme. You always speak of Jesus Christ. Why?" The missionary replied, "Sir, let me ask you a question. What did you have for dinner today?" "Rice," the man replied. "And what did you have yesterday?" "The same thing." "And what do you expect to eat tomorrow?" The questioner replied, "Rice, of course. I can't do without it." The missionary responded, "What rice is to your body, Jesus is to my soul. I can't do without him either."[48]

If your prayers are lackadaisical, lackluster, or even a bit lazy, try something new. Revitalize your prayer life by rehearsing what Jesus means to you. Focus on the Savior. It will be like a shot of Adrenalin to your prayer life. You'll find yourself looking less for answers and more for opportunities to talk with God. Prayer won't be a means to an end; it will be the end itself.

Unblocker #8: Get Off Your Knees

People who are effective in prayer are not super saints. They are not mystical, metaphysical, mysterious, or monastic. They are just regular people—like you and me—who have learned to visit the throne of grace regularly, meaningfully, and joyfully. And they have learned not to stay there. One of the major unblockers to an effective prayer life is to get off your knees and get on your way.

A great deal of answerable prayer depends on what you do *after* you pray. Do you sit back and wait for God to respond? Do you cogitate on whether or not your prayer was biblically correct? Do you question if you have enough faith for God to answer? All those are important, but they should be considered before you pray, not after.

To keep the prayer channels to God open, what should you do after you pray? Grow feet. Having the knees of a camel is only commendable if you also have the feet of a disciple. Don't be a couch-potato prayer warrior. Get up and do something about what you have prayed. Prayer is most answerable when it is accompanied by initiative. Prayer is not a spectator sport. Get into the game.

Suppose you pray that God will encourage your aging friend in an extended care facility. That's good; it's also not enough. God burdened you to pray for your friend; he likely wants to use you to cheer her up as well. This is where you transfer from the Camel-Knee School of Prayer to the Get-Into-Life School of Prayer. Call your friend. Set up a time to visit her. Ask if she would be interested in having you read the Bible to her. Better yet, ask if you may join her for a Bible study. Help her keep those old brain cells functioning. You see, prayer without feet may well be prayer without wings. It's going nowhere.

If you take no initiative to be a part of the answer to your prayers, you may not see an answer either. Effective prayer is always accompanied by initiative. Don't expect one without the other.

What's a Person to Do?

These are the prayer unblockers. They are the things that keep your prayer channels open to God. If you are impressed by God that some of these things can keep your prayer life unblocked, don't hesitate to try them. They have been important to me in my spiritual pilgrimage with God. They can be important to you as well.

Ask God to pinpoint the obstructions in your prayer life just as your doctor would pinpoint the blockages in your arteries. Admit the obstructions exist and are a problem, but also see God as the solution. Then ask him to help you use these unblockers as spiritual angioplasty to open up the highway to his heart and your passageway to prayer.

onclusion

I have been driven many times to my knees by the over-
whelming conviction that I had nowhere else to go.

Abraham Lincoln

The prayer blockers we have investigated are not unique
to those who spring from the pages of the Bible. They
trouble you and me as well. They are not practical anom-
alies, mere deviations from the commonplace. Unfortunately, they tend to become the rule rather than the exception. These prayer blockers hamstring the prayers of the
greatest theologians and the weakest saints. They are the
primary tools Satan uses to keep us from using our primary
weapon—prayer.

Are prayer blockers a serious problem? Think of it this way.
They keep our prayers from reaching God and/or his answers from reaching us. Is that a serious problem? It isn't if
you don't mind your life being powerless, prayerless, and
void of any meaningful relationship with God. If the expression "You don't have a prayer" is what you want for your
life, removing the prayer blockers is of little consequence to
you. But if you want God's ear, if you want his power, if you
want to enjoy the blessing of his perfect will, an unhindered
prayer path to God is crucial.

Spiritual Inventory

These prayer blockers are much more than a list of hindrances to prayer. They should be a checklist against which

you measure your own prayer life. Identifying the problem is the first step to finding a solution. Not all these blockers will be in your path to God, but only you can determine which ones are. That's why it's good to take a spiritual inventory.

Taking a spiritual inventory simply means stepping off the merry-go-round long enough to get a true assessment of how it's going for you in prayer. Do you lack confidence when you pray? Does God seem to be a million miles away? Are you concerned if he is even listening? Do you wonder why God doesn't answer?

You can't answer these questions on the run. Take a few minutes, or more if you need them, to reflect on how meaningful your prayer life is. Are you getting answers or not? Are you spending enough time each day in prayer or not? Ask these questions; don't dodge them.

This is something you should do privately. First, because what blocks your prayers is not likely to be known by others. Second, if you ask someone else to help you with your spiritual inventory, they will almost certainly go easy on you. Given the density of the prayer blockers and the difficulty of going through them, this is not the time to go easy.

Here are some questions you may wish to include in your spiritual inventory:

In the last week, was there any day I simply didn't get around to talking with God? Which day(s)?

In the last week, what specific prayer do I know for sure God answered? What was that answer?

In the last week, excluding saying grace at meals, on average, how many minutes did each of my prayers last?

In the last week, if I multiply the days I talked with God by the number of minutes my conversations lasted each day, on average, how much time did I spend in prayer this past week?

Two final questions:

Am I satisfied with this average?
Is God satisfied with it?

These questions are not designed to send you on a guilt trip. We're just taking an honest inventory. They suggest whether or not your prayer life is adequate to get answers to your prayers. If the inventory reveals inadequacy, you know the prayer blockers are a serious problem to you.

So what's a person to do? Begin by taking each prayer blocker seriously. Use this book as a resource, something to refer to again and again when you suspect a particular blocker is hindering your prayers. View each chapter as part of a checklist. Before you pray, run through the list and ask, "Is Satan using this prayer blocker today?"

God doesn't answer when we:

1. forget to ask
2. cherish sin
3. have a faulty relationship with God
4. have faulty relationships with others
5. need a faith lift
6. harbor an unforgiving spirit
7. ask with the wrong motives
8. ask for the wrong things
9. do not ask in God's will
10. are hindered by satanic interference
11. pray with deniable attitudes
12. quit too soon

Deal with each blocker as a separate hindrance. Don't back down. You have more than adequate resources to remove these hindrances. "You, dear children, are from God and have overcome them, because the one who is in you is greater than the one who is in the world" (1 John 4:4). You can get answers to your prayers if you begin by praying that God will remove the hindrances that block them.

Watch and Pray

Once you have removed the blockers, there's more you can do to get answers to your prayers. Be alert to your enemy. When Jesus and his disciples came to the Garden of Gethsemane on the night he was betrayed, the Savior said to eight of his comrades, "Sit here while I go over there and pray" (Matt. 26:36). Taking Peter, James, and John with him deeper into Gethsemane's darkness, he said to them, "My soul is overwhelmed with sorrow to the point of death. Stay here and keep watch with me" (v. 38).

To the eight the command was "sit and wait." To the three it was "sit and watch." Is there a difference? Absolutely—like the difference between the little gully in your backyard and the Grand Canyon. The Greek word for *watch (gregoreuo)* means to be vigilant, cautious, active. It's the word you would use to warn someone not to allow a calamity to overtake them by surprise.

Jesus used the word in the parable of the ten virgins: "Therefore keep watch, because you do not know the day or the hour" (Matt. 25:13). Paul used it in his concluding challenge to the Corinthians: "Be on your guard; stand firm in the faith; be men of courage; be strong" (1 Cor. 16:13). Peter used it when he advised, "Be self-controlled and alert. Your enemy the devil prowls around like a roaring lion looking for someone to devour" (1 Peter 5:8). And it is used in the warning, "Behold, I come like a thief! Blessed is he who stays awake and keeps his clothes with him, so that he may not go naked and be shamefully exposed" (Rev. 16:15).

While eight disciples only had to wait, three were told to be vigilant and active while they waited. When Jesus returned from praying alone to find the three sleeping, he inquired, "Could you men not keep watch with me for one hour?" (Matt. 26:40). This was not so much a rebuke as it was the kind of question we asked ourselves in the spiritual inventory. Jesus wasn't condemning them; he just wanted them to do some soul-searching. Was it too much to ask Peter, James, and John to be vigilant while they waited for the Lord's return? Jesus didn't think so. He counseled, "Watch and pray so that you will not fall into temptation" (v. 41).

There's good reason to be alert while we pray. Apparently Peter got the point about temptation; he's the one who cautioned us to be alert because our enemy is on the prowl (1 Peter 5:8). Remember, the last thing Satan wants is for us to be successful in prayer. We're invading enemy airspace when we wing our prayers to God (Eph. 2:2). The time of our greatest vigilance should be at the point of our greatest need.

The linkage between vigilance and prayer is like the linkage between frothy milk and espresso coffee. Each is good, but together they are cappuccino. The flavor of each is enhanced by the other. Perhaps your prayers are not answered because you're not alert to Satan's interference. Be careful not to let indolence allow the calamity of unanswered prayer to overtake you. Pray and watch. Watch and pray. Together they are an unbeatable combination.

Successful prayer is never easy prayer. It will take more effort than almost any other Christian activity because Satan hates prayer almost as much as he hates God. If you aren't careful, Satan will convince you that the prayer blockers are immovable and then your prayers will be unanswerable. Don't just pray; be alert and pray.

Pray and Go

Pray and go. It sounds like a fast-food restaurant or a convenience store, doesn't it? Stop and Shop. Park and Eat. Pray and Go. But from what we've just said, we know prayer is not a quick spiritual exercise. It takes time—time alone, time set aside to commune with, reflect on, and receive insight from God.

So what does "pray and go" mean? Just this. When Jesus came to the Garden, he knew his work there would not continue forever. In fact, his real work would soon unfold in a judgment hall, on a skull hill, and in another garden where there was a tomb. Prayer is work, but for most of us it is not *the* work. From the solitude of your study, from the convenience of your kitchen table, from the darkness of Gethsemane, you eventually rise from watching and praying to witnessing and preaching.

When prayer gets tough, the tough get praying. But when the praying is finished, the tough get going. When God communicated with his prayer heroes, often it was to tell them to get going (e.g., Abraham, Gen. 13:17; Moses, Deut. 10:11; Samuel, 1 Sam. 16:12; David, 1 Sam. 23:4; Elijah, 1 Kings 21:17–18; Jeremiah, Jer. 13:6; Ezekiel, Ezek. 3:22; Paul, Acts 9:6). God's message to us today is the same: pray and go.

When Daniel prayed, God sent an angel with the answer. Although that angel was interfered with by Satan, the answer to Daniel's prayer was still delivered on angelic wings. When God's angelic messengers appeared to men in the Bible, often it was to tell them to get going (e.g., Lot, Gen. 19:15; Jacob, Gen. 31:13; Elijah, 1 Kings 19:5–8; 2 Kings 1:3; Joseph, Matt. 2:13; Philip, Acts 8:26; Peter, Acts 12:7). God's message to us today is the same: pray and go.

Perhaps getting answers to your prayers is not as difficult as you think. There are things to do before you pray, while you pray, and after you pray. If you do these things, the likelihood of God hearing you and answering your prayers increases exponentially. Here's what to do:

Before you pray, clear away the roadblocks. Take spiritual inventory. Identify any and all prayer blockers that will hinder you in prayer. Deal with them in faith. Ask God to help. Now you're ready to pray.

While you are praying, be alert to the distractions of Satan. He'll cause your mind to wander, your eyes to get heavy, your phone to ring—anything to keep you from meaningful communion with God. Watch and pray. Ask God to help. Now you're praying with power.

After you have spent sufficient time with God, don't hang around your special place of prayer. Pray and go. Get into life the way you got into prayer. People need you. Put feet to your prayers. Having prayed for God to make you a better servant, go and serve. Ask God to help. Now you are living your prayers.

There's no greater discouragement than unanswered prayer. But remember, there's no greater encouragement than answered prayer. So much of your vitality as a Christian depends on a meaningful prayer life. When God doesn't answer, don't assume anything, but investigate everything. Remove the prayer blockers, be alert to Satan's temptations, and go about your Master's business. If you still don't get an answer, most likely all that is off is your timing. Be patient. Do all that God asks you to do; he'll do the rest.

It's not always our fault when God doesn't answer, but it's never his fault. Prayer blockers are tough and hard, but they crack easily under the hammer of the Holy Spirit. You can get answers from God, but only if you pray.

Notes

Introduction

1. Donald G. Bloesch, *The Struggle of Prayer* (Colorado Springs: Helmers & Howard, 1988), 47.

Chapter 1   We Forget to Ask

2. For more on praying in a biblical way, see Woodrow Kroll, *Empowered to Pray* (Grand Rapids: Baker, 1995).

3. C. S. Lewis, "The Efficacy of Prayer," in *The World's Last Night and Other Essays* (New York: Harcourt Brace Jovanovich, 1960), 8.

4. Lehman Strauss, *Sense and Nonsense about Prayer* (Chicago: Moody, 1974).

5. R. Kent Hughes, *Ephesians* (Wheaton: Crossway, 1990), 250–51.

6. E. M. Bounds, *The Weapon of Prayer* (Grand Rapids: Baker, 1982), 33.

7. Ibid., 13–14.

8. Harold Lindsell, *When You Pray* (Grand Rapids: Baker, 1969), 6.

9. Ibid., 135.

Chapter 4   We Have Faulty Relationships with Others

10. Billy Martin and Peter Golenbock, *Number One* (New York: Delacorte Press, 1980), 117.

11. John Wesley, *John Wesley's Forty-Four Sermons* (London: Epworth, 1975), 348.

12. Richard Sibbes, *The Complete Works of Richard Sibbes,* ed. Alexander Balloch Grosart, vol. 3 (Edinburgh: Nichol, 1862–64), 192.

13. Bill Hybels, *Too Busy Not to Pray* (Downers Grove, Ill.: InterVarsity, 1988), 91.

14. Cameron V. Thompson, *Master Secrets of Prayer* (Madison, Ga.: Light for Living Publications, 1990), 54.

15. Warren W. Wiersbe, *Famous Unanswered Prayers* (Lincoln, Neb.: Back to the Bible, 1986), 11, 13.

Chapter 5   We Need a Faith Lift

16. *Merriam Webster's Collegiate Dictionary,* 10th ed., s.v. "faith."

17. C. S. Lewis, *Christian Reflections,* ed. Walter Hooper (Grand Rapids: Eerdmans, 1967), 42.

18. Lindsell, *When You Pray,* 99–100.

19. Strauss, *Sense and Nonsense about Prayer,* 44.

20. Hugh Thomson Kerr Jr., ed., *A Compend of Luther's Theology* (Philadelphia: Westminster, 1943), 107.

21. Cited in J. Oswald Sanders, *Prayer Power Unlimited* (Chicago: Moody, 1977), 76–77.

Chapter 6   We Harbor an Unforgiving Spirit

22. Thompson, *Master Secrets of Prayer,* 50.

23. Robert Louis Stevenson, "Edinburgh: Picturesque Notes," in *The Works of Robert Louis Stevenson,* vol. 3 (New York: Peter Fenelon Collier, n.d.), 42.

24. R. Kent Hughes, *Abba Father* (Westchester, Ill.: Crossway, 1986), 80.

25. William Hendriksen, "The Commentary of Matthew" in *New Testament Commentary* (Grand Rapids: Baker, 1973), 339–40.

26. Wendell E. Miller, *Forgiveness: The Power and the Puzzles* (Warsaw, Ind.: ClearBrook, 1994).

27. Ibid.

28. Ibid.

29. R. C. H. Lenski, *The Interpretation of St. Mark's Gospel* (Minneapolis: Augsburg, 1964), 496.

Chapter 7   We Ask with the Wrong Motives

30. C. S. Lewis, *Letters to an American Lady,* ed. Clyde Kilby (Grand Rapids: Eerdmans, 1967), 97 (letter dated 28 March 1961).

31. Wiersbe, *Famous Unanswered Prayers,* 10.

Chapter 8   We Ask for the Wrong Things

32. Lindsell, *When You Pray,* 83.

Chapter 9   We Do Not Ask in God's Will

33. Ibid., 86.

Chapter 11   We Pray with Deniable Attitudes

34. *Merriam Webster's Collegiate Dictionary*, 10th ed., s.v. "earnest."

35. Bloesch, *The Struggle of Prayer*, 47.

36. Sibbes, *The Complete Works*, vol. 1, 256.

37. Sanders, *Prayer Power Unlimited*, 82.

38. Bloesch, *The Struggle of Prayer*, 45.

39. Strauss, *Sense and Nonsense about Prayer*, 44.

40. Mickey Bonner, *Brokenness, the Forgotten Factor of Prayer* (Houston: Mickey Bonner Evangelistic Association, 1994), 241–42.

Chapter 12   We Quit Too Soon

41. Helen Smith Shoemaker, *The Secret of Effective Prayer* (Westwood, N.J.: Revell, 1955), 47.

42. Sanders, *Prayer Power Unlimited*, 80.

43. Ibid., 81.

Chapter 13   We Remove the Blockers

44. Alexander Whyte, cited in Sanders, *Prayer Power Unlimited*, 121.

45. C. S. Lewis, *Letters to Malcolm: Chiefly on Prayer* (New York: Harcourt Brace Jovanovich, 1964), 16–17.

46. E. M. Bounds, *Power through Prayer* (London: Marshall, Morgan & Scott, n.d.), 47.

47. William Russell Maltby, *Obiter Scripta* (London: Epworth, 1952), 98.

48. Rosalind Goforth, *Goforth of China* (Grand Rapids: Zondervan, 1937), 109–10.

Woodrow Kroll is president of Back to the Bible in Lincoln, Nebraska, and Bible teacher on the *Back to the Bible* broadcast heard daily around the world.

Before assuming his responsibilities at Back to the Bible in 1990, Kroll spent more than twenty years at colleges and universities training men and women for ministry. He served ten years as president of Practical Bible College in Binghamton, New York. The author of dozens of books, he is a popular speaker at Bible conferences throughout the world.

Kroll received the M.Div. degree from Gordon-Conwell Theological Seminary, and the Th.M. and Th.D. from Geneva-St. Alban's Theological College.